MADE IN ITALY

BY

MARTIN GANI

Martin Gani is the sole copyright holder to this book worldwide

© Martin Gani 2018

Dedicated to lovers of all things Italian

TABLE OF CONTENTS

Prologue

One - Milan, Italy's New York

Two - Money Matters

Three - Italian Politics...Explained

Four - Italian School System

Five - Italian Universities Today

Six - Italian Family in the 21st Century

Seven - Made in Italy

Eight - Silk Artworks of Como

Nine - Truffles and Chocolate

Ten - Le Marche

Eleven - Reading Matters

Twelve - Italy's Cinema Scene

Thirteen - Spumante and Organic Wine

Fourteen - How Green is Italy?

Fifteen - Italy's Tourist Trade

Sixteen - Language Matters

Seventeen - Sanremo...And More

Eighteen - Italian Opera

Nineteen - Alitalia

Twenty - Ravenna, Italy's Most Liveable Province

Twenty -one - Trip to Lazio

Twenty-two - Retirement

PROLOGUE

The aim of this book is to paint a portrait of present-day Italy; titles, Italy As Is, Contemporary Italy, or even, Only In Italy, may have been equally appropriate. It is based on my some three decades of continuous stay in this fascinating country of contradictions as well as numerous local sources, mass media etc. Whenever relevant, and possible, I gave dates, chronology and statistics not to mention Top 10 lists to give proper context and means of comparison.

Judging by statistics borrowed from Google, it appears that Italians have a lot in common with internet users elsewhere; the 10 most frequently clicked websites in 2014 were: google.it; facebook.com; google.com; youtube.com; amazon.it; libero.it; wikipedia.org; eBay. it and repubblica.it. What stands out is the daily newspaper, Repubblica, and libero, an old internet and e-mail provider amazingly still functioning in spite of gmail and yahoo. When it comes to the type of questions Italians asked Google, here we get some interesting information on what Italian internet users are curious about. In the, What is....? category the top question was 'selfie,' placed 5th we have 'virale' (viral) 7th was 'sms' (short message system), despite sending billions of them, many people were apparently wondering what it was short for; in 8th position, like sms 'inps' (acronym for Italy's welfare institute: istituto nazionale previdenza sociale) was investigated; 9th placed was 'ortodosso' (orthodox), what does orthodox mean? millions of people wondered for some reason. In 2016 the words most searched included: idolatria (idolatry), brexit, trust (as in trust fund), schisma (schism), taggare (a hybrid deriving from 'tag' creating the verb: to tag), vegano (vegan) and for some odd reason millions of people wanted to know what podolico meant, for your information this is a grey-skinned cow breed.

Why questions were even more interesting, or bizarre one might say. Four of these why questions were: why do cockroaches invade homes? Why do fleas appear on our bodies? Why do we suffer? and, Why did Peppa Pig die? How to queries were equally intriguing. Number one was, 'barbecue' followed by 'donut' then 'tortellini' and 'malocchio' which can be translated as the evil eye curse. In 2016, the top why enquiries were still on the bizarre side: why does the brazier clog up? Why are cats scared of cucumber?! Why do babies always cry? Why do married men cheat on their wives? And, why do you smoke?

As the Google queries indicate Italians do conform, they use Google, facebook, youtube and wikipedia like the rest of the world but have curiosities that are very unexpected as is their lifestyle, culture, values and attitudes. The twenty-two chapters in this book will explore what makes Italy and its people stand out from the rest of the world. The title Made in Italy refers to what Italians create with much passion be it haute couture, or alta moda as Italians say, status cars like Ferrari, exquisite food and wine from truffles to chocolate to spumante, but also uniquely Italian style politics, education and money matters. Answers are given to questions like: What is Italy's pop music scene like, and opera, where does it come from, which are Italy's top opera houses? What sort of movies do Italians like? What kind of books do they read? What is modern Italian language like, what are its peculiarities, is it still heavily borrowing from English? Is Italian family, marriage institution, values still intact? Where is the best place to live in Italy? How green is Italy? And finally when do Italians retire from work, how much are they paid? Can they live on it? Also included are two travelogues on Le Marche and Lazio regions further shedding light on Italians and their rich culture.

ONE

MILAN, ITALY'S NEW YORK

Milan is often defined Italy's New York (NY) for a good reason. It is Italy's most cosmopolitan city, over 16% of its 1.3-million-strong population is made up of foreigners, more than twice the national average. Today some 400 kebap take-away joints seriously compete with pizza restaurants; the city's Chinese immigrants, hovering around an estimated 80,000 souls, makes it one of the largest Chinese communities in Europe. What's more, there are more consulates in Milan than anywhere else in the world, except NY.

Milan situated deep in the north of Italy is only around 25 miles from Switzerland and enjoys the status of financial capital of Italy and seat of the nation's stock exchange much like NY in USA. Until 1970s every major city in Italy had its own stock exchange but right from the start pragmatic, business-minded Milanese founded the largest companies and listed the largest number of them. Come 1970s, other Italian cities decided they couldn't compete with Milan for sheer size and efficiency and decided to converge there. Today Milan is still the wealthiest city in Italy, generates about 10% of the nations GDP and pays 25% of all the taxes. The Milanese on average earned €34,400 per head in 2016, before taxes, well above the national average of €29,200.

The Milanese have always travelled north to picturesque Lake Como on the border with Switzerland to relax. To make the journey quicker and safer a freeway was built in 1930s linking Milan to Lake Como, the first of its kind in Europe. It was fast but not necessarily danger-free, there were only three lanes, the middle one was used for overtaking by both cars travelling north as well as south. Currently the modern, and safe, dual carriageway has recently been expanded in record time from two to three lanes each way to cope with the increasing traffic.

A few years ago a survey carried out by the famed university, IULM (Istituto Universitario Linguistico di Milano), reported that 74% of tourists coming to Milan associate the city with fashion. True enough together with London, New York and Paris, Italian fashion designers like Giorgio Armani, Prada, Ferré, D&G, Krizia, and Versace, all based in Milan, decide what the rest of the fashion-conscious world should wear. Asked what these well-known designers loved most about Milan, Armani said, "The sense of complicity the city knows how to transmit," D&G: "Discretion, the great efficiency, mental openness," Donatella Versace: "It's not as frenetic as London or New York, it has a human size" Krizia: "The people. They're passionate about their work, creative and concrete." Milan's fashion shopping district with the famed Via Montenapoleone and Via Sant'Andrea has now been joined by Via della Spiga, once mainly inhabited by bakers. Krizia was the first to open shop here in 1974, now Via della Spiga throngs with designer shops. In fact, almost all of Milan's historic heart is today occupied by designer and luxury shops.

Milan as a shopping haven may be a given but not many people realize Italy's shopping history was made here. Galleria Vittorio Emanuele, an extravagant, late 19th-century creation, is one of the planet's earliest, luxury shopping malls rivalled perhaps only by Moscow's G.U.M. for Belle Epoque finery. Nineteenth-century American author Mark Twain visiting Milan was so enchanted by it he declared, "I can happily spend the rest of my life here." That's not all, Italy's first department store, Rinascente, founded in 1918, is still serving customers at their historic seat in the heart of Milan.

Milan has the most publishing houses in Italy and some of the largest bookstores anywhere. The tradition goes back a long time, the first book with Greek characters was printed in Milan in 1476. Milan's daily paper, Corriere Della Sera, is among Italy's top selling newspapers. The book-loving city's Biblioteca Ambrosiana opened in 1609 is considered to be the first public library in Europe. Its treasures include Leonardo's Codex Atlantic, a 1353 edition of Dante's Divina Commedia and a manuscript by the Roman poet Virgil. Ambrosiana is also an art gallery boasting works by the likes of Leonardo, Raphael and Caravaggio.

Culture is serious business in Milan as it is in NY. A brand new museum of modern art, Museo del Novecento, was inaugurated in Dec. 2010 to house 20th-century art, it is bound to rival NY's MOMA. For art pre-dating 20th-century Milan's answer to NY's Metropolitan Museum is, Pinacoteca Brera, where 38 rooms showcase works by Italian greats like Andrea Mantegna, Canaletto, Caravaggio, Lorenzo Lotto as well as works by European masters like Rubens and Rembrandt. There about 60 theatres in Milan too and La Scala, not only Italy's but also one of the world's most famous opera houses, was built here between 1776-1778 and restored by the Swiss-Italian architect Mario Botta between 2002 and 2004. The magnificent construction described as 'Italy's favourite living room,' by the 19th-century French author Stendhal, hosted seven world premieres by Giuseppe Verdi and was the first place in Italy to benefit from Edison's electric light back in 1882. It may not compare to NY's Metropolitan Opera in terms of size, it can seat just over 2,000 spectators against twice as many of Metropolitan but it predates it by nearly 300 years. The original Scala was founded in 1598 and housed in Palazzo Reale (Royal Palace), now used for temporary art exhibitions, before it moved to its current location. Metropolitan was founded in 1880 in Broadway between 39th and 40th Streets and moved to Lincoln Center in 1966. Looking for the 'Old Metropolitan' would be pointless, it was demolished in 1967.

Milan was founded in 6th century BC but unlike most major cities, it is situated in a plain, not on a river or by the sea. However, starting 12th century a canal network, Navigli, connected Milan to lakes Maggiore and Como to the north and the city of Pavia to the south via a series of rivers like Ticino, Olona, Adda and Seveso that traverse Lombardy. This efficient transport system was in use till 1929 when it was decided to inter most of the canals to build roads, today five of the canals are still intact, the most famous being Naviglo Grande, that actually crosses central Milan, it is a tourist haunt lined with colourful cafés, shops and restaurants. In 2016 an extension of this canal, Darsena, was developed and equally became a popular quarter with both the Milanese and tourists. Over the last decade or so studies are being conducted mainly by the Politecnico (university) of Milan to bring the canals back to Milan and create a sort of Venice. Knowing how pragmatic the Milanese are, they'll probably realise the project in the not too distant future. At the beginning the city was named, was named Mediolanum (the land in the middle) by the Romans and served as capital of Western Roman Empire in the 4th century AD. It then became the power base of the Visconti and Sforza dynasties between 14th and 15th centuries. In its long history it was destroyed and rebuilt five times, last after the air raids in 1943. Surprisingly the 15th century castle, Castello Sforzesco, the main tourist attraction, has survived all attacks intact. Walking around the castle museums immersed in history looking at displays of paintings, sculptures, furniture and more, you eventually see people crowding around a sculpture called, Pietà Rondanini, a masterpiece by Michelangelo. Not far off is an unimpressive-looking, frescoed room with a vaulted ceiling known as, Sala delle Asse (hall of the wooden-boards), don't be tempted to walk away immediately. This fresco depicting a labyrinth of leaves and branches, interspersed with white crosses, the Duke Sforzesco's coat of arms, is the work of Leonardo da Vinci. This small hall and the better-known, Last Supper fresco adorning Milan's Santa Maria delle Grazie church, are Leonardo's only surviving works still in their original place of realization. Many people are actually surprised to learn that Leonardo, born in the Tuscan township of Vinci, spent some 25 years of his adult life in and around Milan.

The city's reputation as a place of pragmatic, concrete deeds must have been common knowledge even in Leonardo's time, the eclectic genius in a letter to the Duke applied for a post as 'engineer' not artist. Still today Milan is as famed for its industrial designers as fashion designers. Every year the trade fair devoted to industrial design, Milano Design Week, draws huge crowds and runs parallel to even better-known, Salone del Mobile, which focuses on furniture design Italians are famed for.

Often criticised for doing little to fight pollution, Milan's mayor, Letizia Moratti (replaced by Giuliano Pisapia in May 2011), reacted by doubling pedestrianised areas and charging motorists a fee to enter the city centre which resulted in a reduction of pollution. In 2009 a bike-sharing scheme was introduced. It has been so successful that more and more bikes had to be brought in, late 2014 some 200 bike stands offered around 3,600 bikes to satisfy demand; by autumn 2014 no fewer than 10,000 people were getting around by bike, twice as many compared to 2011, which places Milan among the top five most bike-friendly cities in Europe. If you think Milan has no parks, think again, in the last six years the city's green areas have increased by 247 acres, and over 35,000 trees have been planted. Starting 2012 volunteers around the city have been clearing up dozens of abandoned lots, which normally transform into rubbish tips instantly, and turning them into gardens everyone in the neighbourhood can enjoy; often vegetables are also planted, looked after and the produce shared by all. It's still a long way from NY's central park but Milan is definitely getting greener. The quality of air is getting better as well, at least judging by the dwindling number of cars in the city. Compared to 1990 when some 922,000 cars circulated around the city, come end of 2012 the number dropped by 200,000. Were the Milanese getting wiser, public transport improving or was it the economic recession? Whatever the reason, it's good news for the city considering in the Lombardy region, where Milan is the regional capital, the total number of cars went up by one million to 5.8 million during the same period.

How does Milan compare to other cities around the world? The Economist's global liveability rating for 2015 placed it at 42nd position out of 140 cities considered around the world. Milan scored best (100) in education, its universities such as Politecnico, Bicocca, Statale, Cattolica, IULM and Bocconi are indeed considered quality seats of learning. It's not all good though, on the environment and corruption levels Milan scored poorly. Milanese suburbs are not exactly rose gardens, high-rise housing estates and insufficient development have created neglected areas experiencing social problems including poverty.

Milan was even more frenetic than usual in 2015 as it prepared to host the Universal Expo in 2015 under the theme of, Feeding the World, Energy for Life, where over 140 nations participated. By 2015 Italy had spent around €12 billion on infrastructure alone, the government spent €1.7 billion on the Expo site plus €1.5 billion was invested by the participating countries. According to Letizia Moratti the mayor in 2010 when Milan was assigned the Expo said, "We're getting ready for Expo 2015 fast, the event and our investments are expected to generate €34 billion worth of business and create 70,000 jobs over five years." To which 36,000 voluntary workers must be added to make sure everything runs smoothly. Skyscrapers were going up too, until 2012 the tallest building in Milan was the Pirellone (the seat of city hall) at 127 m (423 feet) inaugurated in 1961, till then the record was held by the cathedral at 107 m (360 feet), the largest Gothic structure in Italy with a capacity for 40,000 and the third biggest church in the world, but the skyline has since changed; Unicredit Tower, soaring to 231 m (758 feet), in 2012 became the tallest building in Italy, several other skyscrapers cropping up alongside it and elsewhere have altered the Italian character of the city, it's not quite Manhattan, there is a sprinkling of skyscrapers not a forest of them as in NY but Milan definitely seems to be moving upwards.

They must have noticed it in NY, a late Jan 2015 issue of New York Times published a list of cities they recommended visiting and put Milan at the top.

The Expo running from May 1st to Oct. 31st, 2015, was expected to attract over 20 million visitors, a third from abroad, and it did, during the 6-month period 1,300 events were held as announced late Jan 2015 including concerts, exhibitions, theatre, fashion shows, entertainment for children as well as food related meetings and conferences on themes like biodiversity, technology in agriculture and how to increase food production to feed the coming generations without damaging the environment. Although most of the events were planned to take place at the Expo site by the townships of Rho and Pero to the north-west of Milan, central Milan itself and other parts of Lombardy region including Lake Como and Lake Maggiore areas were also be involved. Most people arrived at the Rho-Pero railway station which is linked to the Expo site by a bridge. Italy playing the host created a spectacular tree of life sculpture towering in the middle of an artificial pond around it 20 pavilions were erected representing the 20 Italian regions. Besides Italy, 52 other countries built their own individual pavilions, the rest were hosted in 9 clusters. How much did it cost to visit the Milan Expo? If you bought a ticket for a specific date before 1st May, you paid the cheapest rate of €27, an open ticket came to €32 and purchasing one after 1st May cost €39. Advance ticket sales news appeared comforting, by late Jan 2015 around 7.5 million had already been sold.

As always, a year before Expo was to take place the mass media began forecasting serious doubts on whether everything would be ready in time, after all Italy is not famed for its organisational ability; bureaucracy, corruption, organised crime also getting in the way, as widely reported by the Italian media, only catalysed more gloom and doom. Yet, that's exactly what they said last time the Universal Exposition was held in Milan back in 1906. The theme was transport and it had to coincide with the opening of Simplon Tunnel connecting Brig, Switzerland with Domodossola, Italy through the Alps. Began in 1898, in 1905 it was still not ready, but come the Expo inauguration, it was completed, the Simplon Tunnel, nearly 20 km long, was the longest of its kind in the world till 1982. The single-track railway tunnel was matched by a second tunnel that was began in 1912 and completed in 1921. Expo was held in Milan's Sempione Park, still today the city's main park close to the city centre, and attracted just over 4 million visitors; as then also this time come May 1st, 2015 the Expo was ready to welcome the crowds. About 100 days before the inauguration 3,000 workers were covering 20-hour shifts a day to finish the building work, once the interior decorating began the number of workers increased to 4,000. The Expo as expected generated a colossal amount of business and made a substantial contribution to launch Italy's long-awaited economic growth, in other words so much depended on it that, Italy or Italians couldn't possibly let it fail. The event was indeed a sounding success with over 20 million visitors turning up in Milan, spreading the word, as of 2017 Milan is still the most visited city in Italy bringing much tourist revenue to the city. Now that we're onto the economy, let's see how Italy manages its money matters.

TWO

MONEY MATTERS

When Italy's national statistics bureau, ISTAT, announced the unemployment figures for Dec 2014, it was not yet another cold shower; the updated rates stood at 12.9% of working population or around 33.2 million people, this was an improvement compared to a month earlier when 13.2% was out of work, the highest percentage since 1977, in comparison the EU average is about 11%. The reason for the conspicuous rise is of course the on-going economic downturn since late 2008 which led to 25% reduction in Italy's industrial output and a drop of 9% of GDP. Things have improved since then, ISTAT reported that in Nov. 2017 unemployment had dropped to 11.1%.

Meanwhile salaries remained low compared to other major EU countries. A study carried out by Treccani, Italy's famed encyclopedia publishers, in 2013 average earnings of an Italian worker was €1420 a month when German workers earned twice as much and UK and French workers well over €2,000 even in Spain where unemployment is twice that of Italy the workers took home €1850 on average. When it comes to buying power, EU nations spend 68% of their income on essentials like home mortgages, rent, food and transport, in Italy 88% is spent on these basic necessities leaving only 12% disposable income. This doesn't necessarily mean the Italian employers don't pay well, the reason for lower net earnings is also due to high taxes, health and pension contributions that are deducted from Italians' pay checks, as much as half the gross earnings are thus lost. If we also add the indirect taxes such as 22% VAT on most goods and services and high fuel costs not much remains in Italian workers' pockets.

What's most alarming is the youth unemployment, nearly 44% of the under 24, or some 701,000, was out of work in Italy in Dec 2014, other EU nations are equally hit with Greece and Spain having even higher rates but the EU average is a much more manageable 24%. This resulted in tens of 1,000s of Italians moving abroad in search of jobs, according to Fondazione Ismu, a respectable institute carrying out research on inter-ethnic issues, in 2013 officially some 70,000 Italians emigrated mostly to Germany, UK, France and Switzerland; strangely the largest group, 15,000 individuals, was not from the relatively poorer south but the wealthy Lombardy region in the north of Italy. Is this a recent phenomenon? Yes, in 2007 only 4,000 people left Lombardy. By late 2017 here too things have improved, youth unemployment dropped to 35.7% but the number of people leaving Italy actually increased, in 2016 some 124,000 left Italy, again only 50% came from the relatively poorer south the rest was from the wealthier central and northern Italy.

What has the government been doing about this dire crisis? Their best, bearing in mind the national debt in Sep. 2017 was a record €2.3 trillion, as informed by Bank of Italy, that's around 133% of the nation's annual GDP, in EU only Greece has a higher ratio. The high interest rates Italy had to pay to service this huge debt didn't leave much for cutting taxes or injecting cash into the economy. As if that wasn't enough EU imposes on all member nations not to exceed their national budgets by more than 3% which puts further constraints on investment or lending to businesses or home buyers generally depressing the consumer market. The credit crunch continued also in 2013 with loans to families going down by 1.5% and businesses by 6% compared to 2012. But in praise of Italian government it must be pointed out that unlike other EU nations like Portugal, Ireland, Greece, Spain and little Cyprus, whose banking systems collapsed under huge debts and their governments risked defaulting basic payments, Italy did not borrow money from EU or IMF to support the nation's banking system, Italian banks survived the crisis without outside help, none of them going bankrupt, no bailout was necessary.

At a highly critical point late 2011 when interest rates reached unsustainable levels and Italy's 10-year-bonds were paying an incredible 7% interest to attract buyers, Mario Monti replaced Berlusconi as Prime Minister, in Nov 2011 to be exact, and brought in a series of reforms which included raising the age of retirement and introduction of new taxes including a hefty levy on property owners and raising the VAT by a couple of percentages. He also initiated a spending review of state spending to cut costs and continued fighting tax evasion too hoping to put the state finances in order. Tax evasion in Italy is famously endemic, it is calculated that roughly €130 billion a year is not declared to Italy's inland revenue service as revealed by Corte dei Conti (court of audit), other sources claim it's even higher, in any case no other nation in Europe does better. The new government that replaced Monti's in 2013 scrapped the property tax for everyone, rich and poor, but all other taxes and pension reforms stayed.

How is exactly Italian government tackling the devastating recession, credit crunch, unemployment and on-going tax evasion? The austerity measures brought in by Mario Monti have begun taking effect, interest rates on government bonds have come down to manageable levels, as of 2014 they were almost at pre-crisis level, late 2017 they were still as low as can be. According to Bank of Italy, the state owes €91 billion to private companies supplying goods and services. The new government headed by Enrico Letta paid out €20 billion in 2013 and even more in 2014 helped ailing firms unable to get paid by the state. In the words of Minister of Economy, Fabrizio Saccomanni, "In 2013 the state reimbursed €13.5 billion to tax payers." A tiny reduction in overall taxes have also been recorded, all showing signs of economic recovery. Tighter controls have been recovering some €12 billion - €13 billion a year of unpaid taxes. for a few years it was no longer possible make cash payments exceeding €1000, the limit has since been increased to €3,000 but any bank transfers over €10,000 must still be justified and as of 2014 it is illegal to pay rent in cash. A highly sophisticated system called, Redditometro (income measurer) can now legally spy on everyone's bank accounts, keeping tabs on who spends how much and on what, and if the declared income is not compatible with the spending habits, or if a tax payer is spending more than 20% of what he or she officially earns, then they have to justify the extra spending. Late Aug. 2014, Italian media reported a classic case of declared income/spending power incompatibility. The financial police noticed something suspicious in the tax return forms of a wholesale fish merchant in Forlì, central Italy, the gentleman apparently declared annual earnings of €10,000 but he also owned a Ferrari and a Mercedes SUV. Further investigation demonstrated substantial tax evasion and the Ferrari owner was fined €210,000. However, studies carried out by government agencies have realised the so-called redditometro was not worth the effort, the amount of unpaid taxes discovered was disappointingly low and the system is marked for abolishment or downsizing.

War on tax evasion also includes negotiations with European countries such as Switzerland and Luxembourg holding huge sums of Italian money hidden away in their banks to supply information and help catch tax dodgers. In Jan 2015 finally an accord was signed with Switzerland to exchange information on Italians keeping an account there. Italian government also announced those who bring their money back to Italy voluntarily will not face criminal charges provided they pay the inland revenue what they owe. Will Italians listen up to this appeal? Some surprisingly have done, the highly publicized case of famed fashion house, Prada, is a good example. Prada who had moved their legal seat to Luxembourg to pay less tax, legitimately, but continued operating and producing in Italy, which is not legal, admitted to their fault and paid €425 million to avoid criminal charges. In Aug 2014, Giorgio Armani did the same dishing out €270 million; by Nov 2014 the number of companies opting to pay the Italian taxman reached 35; in total they disbursed €2.5 billion.

In defense, tax evaders blame the government for high taxes and bureaucracy that hinder business and bring unbearable burden on Italian companies and the self employed. The confederation of artisans, Confartigianato, in their 2014 annual meeting reported some figures to illustrate the extent of this burden. Over the last 10 years Italian government increased taxes to the order of 3.5% of the nation's annual GDP, higher than anywhere else in Europe. Over the period 28 Apr. 2008 to 28 Mar. 2014, exactly 629 fiscal norms became state law, 72 of them simplified procedures, reduced bureaucracy, unfortunately the remaining 389 complicated things further. For your information in Italy there's a minister of simplification, the only country to have such a ministry as far as I know, alas the minister and his team were unable to simplify much. As to why tax evasion is accompanied by a corresponding increase in taxation is not hard to see, the government has to bridge the gap somehow and the only way to do is to ask for more and more to the state employees and other types of workers and retirees, who can't avoid any taxes, to pay more. The catch 22 situation can only be solved by simplification and reform and adopting the maxim everyone has been shouting, "If we all pay, we all pay less."

The spending review is also beginning to take effect, a number of state-owned assets is to be sold off as well as privatization of state-owned companies like Poste Italiane (Italian Post) whose 30-40% of state shares were to be sold by the end of 2014 but was postponed to 2015, alas. What most Italians look forward to is seeing the politicians earn less, the number of parliamentarians going down by as much as half by the elimination of the Senate and reduction in the number of deputies in the lower house. State funding of political parties will also be phased out gradually, by 2016 they will receive zero euros and have to raise funds like in the USA. Italian stock exchange in 2013 went up by 17% and in 2014 the volume of business transaction rose by 33% and much further still in 2017. Meanwhile the price of petrol halved, euro lost a lot of ground to the US dollar, in early 2014 nearly $1.40 was needed to buy one euro, late 2017 only $1.17 was sufficient, meaning EU exports to USA would cost less and it would be much cheaper for US tourist to visit Italy. In Jan 2015, the Swiss franc no longer artificially devalued by the Swiss Natioal Bank by buying billions of euros, gained 20% against the euro meaning exports to Switzerland instantly became cheaper too. On top of all that European Central Bank announced it would be buying government debts to the tune of €60 billion per month i.e. a lot of cash injection on the way. In short things can only get better for the EU nations including Italy starting 2015, Bank of Italy announced that in 2015 Italian economy grew by over 0.5%, by 0.9% in 2016, and by 1.5% in 2017, much better than everyone expected.. There are other aspects that have been taken into consideration to justify the optimism. ISTAT figures released in Sep 2014 showed that the informal economy generates €200 billion a year, that's 12.4% of the nation's wealth, €15.5 billion of which comes from illegal trade like drug trafficking, prostitution, alcohol and tobacco smuggling, production and sale of fake designer items etc. In other words, in reality, Italians are a little more better off and so is the economy, unofficially anyway.

  How fairly is wealth distributed in Italy? Not that fairly according to the findings of Censis (Centro Studi Investimenti Sociali), a well-known research institute producing statistics on social and economic trends in Italy since 1964, the 10 wealthiest individuals in Italy hold assets worth €75 billion, the same as those held by 500,000 working class families. A broader look reveals that just 2,000 wealthy people have €169 billion between them, not counting real estate, they represent 0.003% of the population but own as much as what 4.5% of the entire population owns. Unsurprisingly, managers and company directors earn, on average,

5.6 times the salary of a worker; over the years the difference has become wider and wider, 20 years ago they earned 3 times the salary of a blue collar worker. The job market over the last 10 years or so have become extremely confusing, numerous types of employment contracts now abound, and only the experts can make head or tails of it. As a result most jobs on offer in any field are not permanent positions and are euphemistically called, 'contratto a termine' a contract for a limited time, which may last from 3 months to a year or more and can only be renewed at the discretion of the employer. This has created a huge mass of young labour force forced to hold on to precarious jobs for years and years. One study reported in Feb 2015 revealed that on average under 30-year-olds were earning about €850 a month. On top of this the government has continued adding paperwork rendering the process of employing someone unduly complicated. Journalist Beppe Severgini writing for Corriere della Sera gave a perfect example: "We needed an intern at my office, it took 12 authorisations to actually employ the chosen candidate;" in other words 12 layers of bureaucracy.

    Meanwhile Prime Minister Enrico Letta was replaced by 39-year-old Matteo Renzi in Feb 2014 who announced a long list of reforms and tax reduction, he stood by his promise and diverted €80   a month to some 10 million low-middle income workers starting May 2014 to help boost the economy via increased, however modest, consumer spending. Renzi government brought in new employment legislation with an English name: Job Act which should simplify the job market rules as well as giving employers incentive to hire more; the state will be paying the social security contributions for these new employees for three years to help reduce hiring costs for companies. A highly controversial legal point, known as articolo 18, was modified which means employers can dismiss employees they're unhappy with or during economic hardship, something they couldn't do before, it all had to be decided by a judge. However, no worker can be fired on grounds of racial, religious, sexist etc. discrimination, Renzi's government hopes this will encourage more hiring and bring in investment from abroad too. With the new law employees will have increasingly more rights and job security and by the end of three years they must be given unlimited work contracts. Renzi also managed to pass legislation to abolish Italy's 110 provinces that will in time simplify administration and reduce public spending, as well as to reform the Senate to become a non-elected body whose members, reduced in number to about a third, will get no salaries. Renzi is intent on making life easier for the working population, for instance starting 2015 millions of employees won't have to fill out complicated tax returns, it will be automatically done for them by the state, and any mistakes in them will no longer be the responsibility of the tax payers. Mistakes intentional or otherwise are punished by law, inflicting fines on the 'poor' citizen bewildered by the complexity of Italy's taxation system. Nobody is really able to fill out a tax return form, companies and the self-employed have accountants, the rest of the population goes to fiscal assistance centres known as CAF and for a fee they get advice and have their forms filled out and sent off.

Is the Italian government headed by young, ambitious Matteo Renzi going to be able to simplify life, bring in essential reforms in time to improve the economy, ease taxation, reduce tax evasion bring in prosperity, fairer wealth distribution and truly make life easier for all Italians? It will take a lot effort, skill and political juggling, but first let's take a look at how Italian politics work.

THREE

ITALIAN POLITICS... EXPLAINED

Attempting to explain Italy's political system is a massive undertaking. Whereas in other countries there is a small number of parties but politicians come and go, in Italy political parties frequently change names, manifestos and colour but the politicians virtually stay the same. What follows is the very current political situation in Italy starting the latest general elections held in Feb. 2013. As you will soon realise, forming a government, after the elections, as it happens in most countries, is a complex issue in Italy, very complex. Between 2011 and 2014 four different Prime Ministers, hence governments, ran the country.

The general elections were held over two days, not one day like everywhere else, on Feb. 24 - 25, 2013, Italian president Giorgio Napolitano's first comment on the outcome was, "Complicated." No party or a coalition of parties had won a clear majority in both the Senato (the senate) and the Camera (the chamber of deputies) which together form the Italian parliament made up of 630 deputies and 315 senators; in comparison US elects 435 members to the House of Representatives and only 100 senators.

Although the coalition of parties led by Partito Democratico (PD) secured 340 deputies in the Camera, giving them a clear majority, they couldn't do the same in the Senato where they only had 123 senators, they needed at least 158. The only option was to form a coalition with one or more of the other winners: Popolo della Libertà (PDL) led by Silvio Berlusconi; Movimento 5 Stelle (M5S); and Scelta Civica, a group led by Mario Monti whose caretaker government of technocrats had been running the country since Nov. 2011. Monti's pension reforms and other measures like the introduction of a property tax and raising the VAT from 20% to 22% avoided Italy going bankrupt and brought the state finances, and interest rates Italy pays on its colossal national debt, under control. Hoping to ride on his success, Monti was hoping to attract a substantial percentage of the electorate but he only managed around 9% of the vote and elected 19 senators, not enough to help PD to get a majority. Bearing in mind Monti was the only one willing to stand by PD, this came as a blow to PD who simply refused to look to the arch enemy Berlusconi for support. Their only hope was to call on M5S, unfortunately, their leader Beppe Grillo turned down any offer of collaboration with any of the parties accusing them of corruption and mismanagement of taxpayers' money. The M5S proposed to form of a government alone, but with only 25% of the votes they have no majority in any of the houses.

Despite the stalemate, three weeks after the vote, the parliament had to officially elect a speaker for the Senato and Camera, which it miraculously did, especially in the Senato, thanks to a dozen or so defections from M5S who disobeyed their leader and voted for a candidate proposed by PD; both speakers: Laura Boldrini (Camera) and Pietro Grasso (Senato) were newcomers who had never before been a member of any party, one reason the M5S voted for them to avoid the election of other veteran politicians. Boldrini represented Italy in UN high commission for refugees; Sicilian Grasso was, since 2005, the national head of public prosecutors fighting organized crime. A week after the election of the speakers, Pier Luigi Bersani, the leader of PD at the time, was officially appointed by Napolitano to consult other party representatives to see if he could from a stable government; as expected, he couldn't convince M5S to join him. Curiously the PDL was the only party willing to support PD and form a grand coalition of all parties to address the economic issues plaguing Italy and bring in some urgent reforms. PD insisted PDL's proposals were mostly incompatible with the reforms PD wanted to tackle including changes to the judicial system which would render individuals indicted for any crimes ineligible to Italian parliament, and bring in legislation to solve the conflict of interest issues. Both are detrimental to Berlusconi who is facing a series of charges brought against him and is frequently summoned to law courts to defend himself. Regarding his media empire of TV channels, newspapers, books and magazines, no regulation of this blatant conflict of interest exists and both PD and M5S want to put an end to it.

Given the exceptional situation, everyone awaited Napolitano to come up with a solution, and the president exceptionally drew up a list of 10 names (prominent jurists and economists), locally called 'saggi' (wise men), to single out the most urgent economic, social and state organization issues to deal with and advise the newly elect parliament to act on them. The saggi began work on Apr. 2nd and were only given 10 days to come up with ideas. Napolitano was running out of time as his term as president would expire on May 15th and according to Italian constitution a new president had to be elected by Apr. 15th. Meanwhile the Monti government continued handling the day to day running of the country.

General elections in Italy are held every five years but the president of the republic is elected every seven years. Anyone at least 18 years old, that's 47 million Italians, have the right to vote for deputies to the Camera; for the Senato you have to be over 25 to vote, around 42 million Italians make up this more mature group. At the Feb. 2013 elections turnout was 75%, about 5% less than in 2008. A candidate for the Camera must be at least 25 years old, the same as for the US House of Representatives, but the Senato requires candidates to be at least 40 years old, for the US Senate it's enough to have reached the age of 30. Starting 2002 Italians living abroad can participate in the vote by registering with AIRE (Anagrafe Residenti Italiani All'Estero). According to Italian Ministry for Internal Affairs there are 3.5 million registered

Italians living abroad, 171,225 in US and some 600,000 in UK. The number is bound to be much bigger, not everyone registers with AIRE.

The election of the Italian president, the head of state, varies significantly from the US or France for instance. He, or she, in Italy has to be at least 50, in USA 35 years of age is sufficient, in Argentina 35 and in France only 18. In the US, Argentina and France the president is elected by the people, in Italy by the 945 members of parliament, the lifetime senators (currently 6) and 58 regional councillors, every one of 20 regions sends three electors, Valle d'Aosta being very small sends just one, in total 1007 electors were to vote for candidates proposed by the political parties. Two thirds majority (672 votes) is required to elect the president, but if after three rounds of voting there's still no winner, a simple majority (504 votes) is sufficient.

On Apr. 18th the 1007 electors assembled in the Camera; PD proposed Franco Marini, endorsed by PDL and Monti's Scelta Civica, but he did not get enough votes. The M5S proposed 80-year-old Stefano Rodotà. Three rounds of voting didn't produce a winner; for the fourth round, PD came up with Romano Prodi (not approved by PDL), but 101 deputies and senators of PD, out of a total 494, refused to vote for Prodi effectively blocking his election. Bersani accusing his party of anarchy and feudalism resigned. After five rounds of voting, there was still no winner. In a desperate attempt Napolitano was 'begged' to agree for a second term which he reluctantly did getting re-elected with a stunning 738 votes. Napolitano swiftly appointed 46-year-old Enrico Letta, the second in command at PD, to form a coalition government composed of PD, PDL and Scelta Civica. On Apr. 27 Letta managed to put together a team of 21 ministers, seven of them women. Finally on Apr. 28, 62 days after the elections, Italy's 62nd government was sworn in.

Things didn't really run smoothly, on Feb. 14th, Letta lost a vote of confidence and was replaced by Renzi as prime minister.

His reign lasted till Dec. 4th, 2016 when a referendum was held to change the constitution and essentially reduce the number of parliamentarians virtually abolishing the senate leaving only 100 non-elected members with little executive power. Moderate Renzi meanwhile had much opposition from the more left-leaning members of his own party who campaigned against him arguing the senate was a control body that ensured democracy and proper lawmaking. Renzi at some point also put his own career as politician on the line declaring he would step down if the referendum failed. This was more than an invitation for all the opposition and the PD's left-wing members and supporters to vote against, not so much for the issues in the referendum but just to oust Renzi, 65% of the electorate turned out, Renzi lost, 59% said no to the reforms he had proposed. Renzi, as promised, stepped down as prime minister and was replaced by low key, Paolo Gentiloni. PD began experiencing turmoil within the party that was only resolved by primaries to elect a new leader, in May 2017, Renzi attracting over two million votes was again elected party leader. The lefties of the party increasingly turned anti Renzi accusing him of abandoning the values of the centre-left and leaning more towards the centre and a number of renowned member like Massimo d'Alema and Pier Luigi Bersani left PD forming a new party, Movimento Democratici Progressisti (MDP) and chose a new leader Pietro Grasso. Meanwhile, the former mayor of Milan, Giuliano Pisapia, put together a party of his own and tried to unite the centre-left parties, it proved too difficult, he couldn't find common ground between PD and MDP and on Dec. 6th he threw in the towel and announced he wouldn't be standing for election, his party joined forces with MDP which changed name becoming, Liberi e Uguali (free and equal).

    Meanwhile, a new election law, Rosatellum, came into force in 2017 whereby two thirds of parliament would have proportional representation and a third would be elected with the first-past-the-post system. This opened the doors to coalition of parties big and small as a way of reaching a majority. To everyone's surprise 81-year-old Silvio Berlusconi returned to mainstream politics forming a coalition with right-wing, anti-immigration, populist, Lega Nord, vociferously run by Matteo Salvini, and another right-wing, nationalist party, Fratelli d'Italia, led by Giorgia Meloni. Berlusconi's coalition won the elections in Sicily held in Nov. 2017 to elect a governor and the regional council members, Sicily an autonomous region elects its own parliament. PD scored relatively poorly, coming third most voted party, showing yet again arguing against one another with the mass media reporting every word, and blatant division within only damages a party, the other contenders M5S came second. On Dec. 28th, 2017 President Mattarella dissolved parliament and announced new elections employing Rosatellum for March 4th, 2018.

What are the duties and responsibilities of the Italian head of state? It is very different from the US, or French, president who hold executive power, run the country with the help of the Congress, the Italian president is essentially a figure head with little executive power but nevertheless has many important duties. He scrutinizes every law passed by the parliament, making sure it is compatible with Italian constitution, and then puts his signature to it. He has the power to dissolve parliament, appoint a new one, as he did with Mario Monti, can appoint up to five lifetime senators, and can pardon a convicted prisoner, there's no death penalty in Italy, so it isn't about saving someone's life. Italy's equivalent of US president is, Presidente del Consiglio, or the Prime Minister (PM), this is usually the leader of the winning political party at the elections.

How many parties are there in Italy? Numerous. At the Feb. 2013 general election some 120 parties took part, many of them in coalition with bigger parties. To take part in the election, new parties i.e. those who have never had a deputy or senator elected, must collect at least 160,000 signatures to qualify. As the

2013 elections were called early, it was enough to collect 30,000 signatures, hence the huge number of parties. To give an example, the PD led a coalition of four parties for the Camera and nine for the Senato, and the PDL nine and twelve parties respectively. It must however be pointed out that most of the parties participating did not elect a single deputy or senator because a party had to attract at least 4% of the national vote and a coalition at least 8% to get anyone elected to the Camera, for the Senato it was even more difficult, a party needed 8% and a coalition 20% of the vote to elect senators. The following six parties received around 90% of the vote. Who are they, where do they stand and how do they intend to tackle the many economic and social issues Italy faces today? The main problems are: unemployment, the huge national debt, economic growth, bureaucracy and social issues like increasing poverty and assimilation of immigrants.

Partito Democratico (PD)
After the resignation of Pier Luigi Bersani, PD chose Guglielmo Epifani as interim leader and was later replaced by Matteo Renzi; it is one of Italy's biggest parties, politically centre-left, alone it got 25.4% of the vote in the Camera and 27.4% in the Senato. At the 2014 European Parliament elections PD attracted the most votes, nearly 41%. In line with the other major parties, PD proposed to halve the number of parliamentarians and abolish state financing of parties. Both proposals were accepted and have been approved by the parliament. Alas, as mentioned above, the referendum to halve the parliamentarians and abolish the Senato failed. Between 1996 and 2006 state funding of parties increased 10-fold to €470 million, for the 2013 elections this was cut to €190m. It may seem a lot but during the US presidential elections $5.8billion was spent (Source: Time Magazine), the only difference being in the US it didn't cost a cent to the tax payers. PD strongly wants to oppose tax evasion by drastically reducing the informal, cash economy, by making it obligatory to pay for

goods and services exceeding €300 - €400 by using only electronic money; it was never approved, on the contrary the limit for cash payments was increased from €1,000 to €3,000. Again in line with other parties, they propose to speed up payments by the state to private companies for goods and services rendered. PD is also determined to regulate conflict of interest situations and allow the children born in Italy to foreign parents to automatically obtain Italian nationality once they finish primary school, as of December 2017, nearly the end of the line for this government as new general elections are announced for Mar. 4th, 2018, no such law was passed bringing much criticism to Renzi and his party for not keeping this important promise.

Popolo delle Libertà (PDL)

Led by veteran Silvio Berlusconi, PDL was Italy's major centre-right party whose main focus is the economy; they wanted to immediately repeal the unpopular municipal property tax, IMU, introduced by Monti, as well as gradually eliminating the dreaded regional levy, IRAP, all businesses must pay. In response Renzi's government has reduced IRAP but did not eliminate it. Renzi's government did abolish IMU. They proposed to reduce the overall annual state spending of €800 billion by 2% a year. To help decrease youth unemployment, they have proposed tax exemption for employers who hire them, again Renzi's Jobs Act has done exactly that. PDL attracted around 22% of the vote. In 2014 PDL split into two factions, Forza Italia run by Silvio Berlusconi who left the coalition with PD, and Nuovo Centro Destra (new centre-right) run by Angelino Alfano, who decided to continue supporting PD. Simultaneously a pact known as, Patto del Nazareno, was born between Berlusconi and Renzi to cooperate in achieving reforms they both approved. Renzi needed the votes of Berlusconi's Forza Italia in the senate to pass laws.

Movimento 5 Stelle (M5S)

Founded by Genoese stand-up comedian Beppe Grillo and Gianroberto Casaleggio, M5S is aiming at revolutionizing Italian politics. They attracted just over 25% of the vote and do not trust, support or want to collaborate with any of the traditional parties; in parliament they only vote for laws they approve of. They demand all state funding of parties to be abolished (M5S has never accepted money from the state) and insist all politicians should only serve a maximum of two terms, like the US president. Their other proposals range from controversial e.g. holding a referendum to maintain or abandon euro as the national currency, to utopian e.g. guaranteeing a salary for all citizens and free internet for everyone. M5S started and continues to communicate via internet, their deputies and senators till recently did not talk to the press and never participated in current affairs programs or talk shows on TV anyone caught doing so is severely criticized and/or expelled. Realising this was a mistake, they now behave like everyone else airing their views on the media whenever they can. Official communications still go through the two speakers, one from the Senato and another from the Camera. M5S was criticized for its obstructionist attitude towards the formation of a government and is now the main opposition party with no sympathy for any PD-led government. Despite scoring poorly at the 2014 European elections, they're one of the three main parties in Italy and still insist on not forming a collation government making it hard for them to actually govern the country. Like Lega Nord, they have an ambiguous position on EU membership and especially euro as currency, their official candidate for the Prime Minister's job, Luigi di Maio, announced holding a referendum to abandon euro a possibility though ruled out any referendum to leave the EU.

Lega Nord (northern league)

It was born in early 1990s in the north of Italy in protest to government inefficiency, corruption and waste of money the rich northern regions sent to the poor south. It is now headed by 1973-

born Matteo Salvini. Lega Nord's main aim is a federalist system of government strongly opposing immigration. Currently two big, and wealthy, regions, Lombardia and Veneto are governed by Lega Nord who were allied with PDL in the former Berlusconi government, and the Feb. 2013 elections, obtaining just over 4% of the vote. Lega Nord at the time was focusing on the creation of a macro-region in northern Italy, and keeping 75% of taxes paid in the north. Nobody is talking about this ambitious project now. The exponential rise in immigration to Italy over the past few years brought much sympathy to Lega Nord whose electorate base has meanwhile increased, it is likely to receive a double digit percentage of the votes in the coming general election in spring 2018 and signed a coalition agreement with Berlusconi's Forza Italia and Giorgia Meloni's Fratelli d'Italia to form a centre-right government. In case of electoral success to form a government, who is going to be the PM is not certain although Salvini has self-promoted himself for the post many times arguing if his party gets the most votes in the coalition, he should be given the job.

Sinistra Ecologia Libertà (SEL)

An offshoot of Italy's communist party, SEL is led by the openly homosexual former governor of Puglia, Nichi Vendola; it was allied with PD at the Feb. 2013 elections attracting around 3% of the vote. The speaker of the Camera, Laura Boldrini is a SEL deputy. The SEL's focus is in line with those of PD and include environmental protection and legalising gay marriages in Italy. However they strongly opposed a coalition government with PDL and hence, like M5S, did not approve of Letta's government but said their opposition would be constructive. They also strongly criticised Renzi's accord with Berlusconi.

Scelta Civica (SC)

Put together by Mario Monti, it consists mainly of economists and academics many of whom served as technocrats with Monti during his 15-month caretaker government that led up to the general elections in Feb. 2013. SC obtained some 9% of the vote.

All parties agree the election system at the time, disparagingly called, *Porcellum*, must be changed. It was introduced in 2006 to guarantee a clear majority for the winning party, or coalition of parties, by awarding them 55% of the seats in the Camera; in the Feb. 2013 elections the coalition of parties led by PD was the winner; although they only obtained 29.5% of the vote, with the Porcellum system this lead was extended to 55%. However, in the Senato there's no such reward of extra seats, hence, despite coming first, the PD coalition was unable to have a majority in the Senato. The other hotly contested aspect of the Porcellum is that the citizens can't choose which candidate to vote for. The candidates are appointed by the party leaders and automatically those occupying the top positions on the lists get elected. Before 2006, the voters could choose a name from a list of candidates giving them some power over who got elected. Come 2014 Italy's constitutional court declared Porcellum unconstitutional. A new election law had to be formulated, PD proposed: *Italicum*. After much ado it was finally accepted but had to be discussed in detail before the final voting that would make it a law. Much opposition ensued from more left-leaning members of PD itself who were also highly suspicious of Renzi's accord with Berlusconi. It was to be a proportional system of voting, the party attracting at least 40% of the vote was to get a premium i.e. awarded extra seats to guarantee a majority, similar to Porcellum in a way. To elect a parliamentarian a party had to obtain at least 3% of the vote. If no one achieved 40%, run-off elections were to be held between the two most successful parties. The parliamentarians could not agree on Italicum and a new version of the law had to drawn; after extenuating debate, analysis and controversy a new election system called Rosatellum was finally voted by the parliament in 2017. The new law called requires each party to get at least 3% of the vote and a coalition 10%.

Here's a brief rundown on how things have evolved since Dec 2013 when Matteo Renzi won the primaries and replaced Luigi Bersani as leader of PD. In Feb 2014 he took over from Enrico Letta as the new Italian PM and got down to work; appointed women ministers for half the positions available including defence, foreign affairs, health, education and public administration, his right-hand man is a woman too, Maria Elena Boschi, thirty something Boschi is also the Minister for Reforms. Renzi came under criticism for deposing Letta, even by some in his own party, after all Renzi wasn't elected and obtained the PM position by an inside job, by elbowing his way to the top job. What most failed to realise was that Renzi was increasingly getting popular with everyone regardless of political colour. His good communication skills, ambitious reform projects, giving a lot of space to women politicians, were received well by the business community and conservative voters as well, after Berlusconi and Monti there really was no-one else who inspired much confidence in Italians. In May 2014, elections were held again this time for the European Parliament, it was also a test to see where parties stood as far as Italian citizens were concerned. Berlusconi after 13 years of trials and appeals was charged with tax evasion and sentenced to do community service for a year (4 hours a week) at an old people's home in Milan, his passport was confiscated and was banned from engaging in any political activity, hence his party, Forza Italia, didn't seem likely to win the most votes despite a strong following. Grillo's M5S ran a truly aggressive campaign attacking Renzi's government at every opportunity, undermining any effort he made to improve things, and continued, obstinately not to cooperate. This must have frightened Italians, M5S criticised a lot but proposed little, predicting gloom and doom all the way to the poll day. By late Jan 2015 36 of their parliamentarians had either been expelled or left the movement of their own accord disagreeing with the policies of their leader. The result was almost a landslide victory for Renzi who received nearly 41% of the vote,

M5S came second with around 21% and Forza Italia third with about 17%. The only part made a gain was Lega Nord with 6% ironically campaigning for abandonment of the euro as national currency for Italy. Renzi was now recognised as a true leader and deserved to be the PM. In case you're wondering, Berlusconi's Bunga Bunga parties which made headlines around the world was investigated by magistrates bearing in mind sex with a minor, the Moroccan girl nicknamed Ruby Rubacuori, was one of the charges brought against Berlusconi. He was also accused of abuse of power because at one stage Ruby was arrested by the police for theft in 2010, the officer in charge received a phone call from Berlusconi asking him to let the girl go, she is a niece of Egyptian president Mubarak's, he explained, so Ruby went free. In July 2014, after four years of court battle Berlusconi was acquitted of all charges: not guilty.

In Jul 2014 Italy took over the 6-month rotating presidency of EU and Renzi spent a lot of time trying to convince the EU leaders to introduce more flexibility, less austerity, more investment to help increase jobs. When the EU presidency ended towards the middle of Jan 2015, 89-year-old Italian President Napolitano announced his resignation as he had said he would. Renzi rolled up his sleeves, consulted all other party leaders, everyone suspected the Patto del Nazareno with Berlusconi would result in choosing a candidate that would suit Berlusconi. Taking everyone by surprise Renzi proposed 73-year-old Sergio Mattarella, a Sicilian judge from Palermo as the only candidate, Berlusconi objected accusing Renzi of breaking their agreement, SEL and left-leaning PD faction cheered. On the fourth round of voting on the morning of Jan 31st, 2015, Mattarella was elected Italy's new president with 665 votes for the next seven years.

Back to real life, Renzi's team swiftly announced sweeping reforms aimed at reducing taxes, demoting the role of the Senato to a non-elected consultative body alone 95% made up of regional councillors and the rest former presidents of state and the senators they nominate, simplifying public administration and introduced the Jobs Act, to reform employment rules, regulations and reduce the huge number of contract types to render hiring an apprentice or intern easy, inexpensive and simple. Amazingly some concrete results have come by, apart from the €80 bonus a month, laws were passed that effectively reduced the Senato to 100, unpaid members. In public administration steps were taken to simplify life by computerising a lot of procedures, and offering more and more online services, the salaries of managers running state-owned companies, like the railways, the national carrier Alitalia, and energy company, ENI, had a cap introduced. Starting Apr 2014, no manager can earn over €240,000 before taxes. In all areas of public administration, a spending review is in course, actually it had already started even before Monti, that should improve efficiency and save tax payers' money and invest it in infrastructure to create jobs starting with upgrading of school buildings for which the government earmarked some €10 billion to spend over four years. Now that we're on the subject of schools, let's take a look at how Italy's school system functions.

FOUR

ITALIAN SCHOOL SYSTEM

As everything else in Italy, the school system is equally complex and in need of improvement. Every education minister desperately tries to introduce reforms that are hard to implement and often get lost in red tape and endless debate. Although a series of reforms down the decades has produced some modernisation, it has been much too slow to respond to the needs of the society and the type of skilled or specialised workforce the employers seek. In the end little of what really matters, teaching methods, efficiency and teacher employment methods, have lagged behind. For instance an army of supply teachers on temporary contracts, lasting from a few weeks to a year, find themselves in a new establishment often in a new city every year. Ageing teaching staff naturally resist change; according to OECD (Organisation for Economic Co-operation and Development) representing 35 countries around the world, in 2013 the average age of an Italian teacher was 49, higher than in most other countries, and the principals were on average 57 years of age, again higher than most other countries. A huge gender gap also prevails, in 2013 nearly 79% of teachers, and over 55% of school principals, were women. Primary school teachers work 18 hours a week plus 80 hours a year but these extra hours are spent on meetings, lesson preparation and administration swallowing up precious time that would be better spent on education rather than bureaucracy.

    Compulsory primary education in Italy began in 1859 at a time when 80% of the population was illiterate; it took half a century to halve, today, also thanks to educational TV programs starting late 1950s, literacy has reached nearly 99%. In 1923 it was made compulsory for children to attend school till the age of 14, three years more than before. Incredibly this age limit remained till the year 2000 when education minister Luigi Berlinguer raised it to

16 years of age. In 1965 for those unwilling go on to university but willing to learn a trade of some sort, two types of technical schools were introduced: Istituto Technico which trained teenagers for office work e.g. accounting, administration, tourism, and Istituto Professionale which focused on more practical subjects like handicraft, engineering, technical assistance.

In recent years more and more effort has been made to reorganise the system, raise standards but also to spend more efficiently. Education minister Mariastella Gelmini under Berlusconi government in 2008 made a serious attempt following the revelation of disturbing statistics. In a survey carried out by OECD the year before informed that Italian secondary schools came 28th out of 30 countries considered. Italy's official statistics body, ISTAT, informed that in 2007, some 26% of the population had only received primary school education and only 32% held a high school diploma. A study by University of Milan published in Nov. 2006 found that out of a 1000 kids starting primary school, only 666 would eventually obtain a high school diploma; this abandonment, which translates to one in three, is twice the rate of other European Union member states and costs the state €2.5 billion a year. Paradoxically Italian schools have 9.3 teachers per 100 pupils, the OECD average is 5.9, in short Italy spends more to get less. Overall spending on education has however gone down; in their annual report in 2014, OECD found that only 9% of Italy's public spending went to primary and secondary education in 2012 compared to 13% OECD average. They also disturbingly noted that 14% of 17-year-olds abandoned school in Italy, that's 4% more than OECD average. But it's not all bad news, reading and maths skills of 15-year-olds have improved. More recent statistics reported by Eurostat say that in 2014 Italy earmarked 7.9% of public spending for education only Greece spent less in EU. Meanwhile, the latest statistics published in 2017 again by Eurostat showed that in 2015 Italy spent 4.0% of its GDP on education compared to 4.9% EU average.

How did Gelmini try to raise standards and rationalise spending? Some basics: Italian school today is divided into three segments, primary school (6-11), middle school (11-14) and high school (14-19). According to the ministry of education in 2012 there were around 626,000 teachers occupying permanent posts (down to 601,000 in 2017) in Italy and the average number of pupils per class stood at around 21. Starting 1990 primary schools have enjoyed three teachers per two classes instead of one teacher per class. By going back to one-teacher system plus an English and religion teacher where needed, reducing the number of schools in areas where there is a significant drop in the number of pupils or having them share one administration, Gelmini wanted to reduce the number of employees by about 130,000, of which around 87,400 would be teachers, and eventually save €8 billion over the following three years. She said the teachers were too many, and earned too little, the reforms would increase their income, status and motivation, a third of the money saved would be re-invested in schools not only for salaries but also for equipment and materials; true enough Italian teachers earn much less than their counterparts in other developed nations; in Italy a middle school teacher with 15 years experience earns $31,890 per annum before taxes, the average in the OECD is $40,682. Streamlining would also affect middle and high schools where for instance standard teaching hours would be reduced by about 10%. In 2017 number of teachers occupying permanent post was reduced to 601,000 but were helped by nearly 50,000 supply teachers.

Gelmini also intended to do some social engineering by making it compulsory to wear a school uniform in primary schools hence eliminating social differences reflected in expensive designer clothes and shoes Italian kids love to wear, but the final decision is left to the school principals, as well as re-introduce a mark in 'condotta' (behaviour) in middle and high schools to improve discipline, those who get less than 6 out of 10 in 'condotta' would risk failing the year. Thousands took to the streets, disrupted classes in schools and occupied universities to protest against the reforms arguing the aim was only to reduce spending not increase quality of teaching.

How did Gelmini propose to have fewer, more cost-effective and better teachers? Starting 1997, you need a university degree to teach but currently 324,000 teachers, around 54% holding a permanent post, don't have a degree. Of the 247,000 or so primary school teachers, over 82% are high school graduates. Potential teachers are put on a 'graduatoria,' a sort of 'waiting list,' compiled following a 'concorso' a public admission test open to all, and those scoring high enough are put on the list, and become temporary supply teachers, in time, or by doing specialisation courses they gain points and move up the 'graduatoria,' in 2007 there were 300,000 teachers on the list but only 190,000 of them were active in the system and taught on and off. Four supply teachers out of ten moved to another school in Sep. 2007 hindering didactic continuity. With the reforms, effective from Sep. 2009, retiring teachers wouldn't be replaced, the 'graduatoria' would be frozen, schools would gradually gain more autonomy and recruit teachers from a provincial 'graduatoria' and evaluate their performance over a year before offering permanent positions. Three career grades, 'iniziale' (beginner) 'ordinario' (ordinary) and 'esperto' (expert) would be created so as to simplify the system as well as motivate teachers who would also earn more as they move up the scale resulting in fewer but better qualified teachers with better salaries, more stable jobs working in better equipped institutions. As expected these good intentions only partly became reality. The three career grades idea simply faded into history, salaries remained unchanged and the graduatoria became even longer, the daily, La Stampa, reported that in Aug 2014, there were 500,000 hopeful teachers on stand-by on the graduatoria. Schools have gained little autonomy, just as before when a post is available, they can't choose the best qualified, most experienced, most appropriate candidate for the job, they're sent the next available person on the waiting list, the graduatoria.

Five years on standards don't seem to have gone up much either. According to OECD sponsored PISA (Program for International Student Assessment) whereby the performance of 15-year-olds from 65 countries were assessed in maths, reading skills and science, Italy came 32nd, the scores of Italian teenagers were slightly below the average but they did better than USA, Russia and Sweden for instance.

In OECD's latest report published in Dec 2014 the number of hours 15-year-olds spend on homework was looked at. The Russians with 9 hours a day topped the list with Italians coming second with 8.7 hours. The average for the OECD nations was 5 hours. Hard work however did not translate to achievement, Italian, or Russian, teenagers did not perform better than others. OECD analyst, Francesca Borgonovi, on the pages of Italian daily, Sole 24 Ore, commented, "Italian adolescents lack motivation, they see school as something distant from their and their family's everyday life, teenagers, and parents, don't see school as a means to social mobility or career success; the teachers on the other hand are discouraged and frustrated as they don't see any career prospects, meanwhile on-going school reforms lack any long-term strategies to tackle and promote social change rather than endure it." In a typical setting Italian parents are involved in the long hours of homework doing and help their children. This of course depends on the family, the educated, higher-income families will tend to show much more interest in their children's school performance. To bridge the gap Borgonovi suggested the school should help the underprivileged to improve by offering them extra classes and not leaving it to the family, reducing the amount of homework would also be helpful. Introduction of real life job experience as done in countries like Poland, Singapore and Switzerland should also be useful. Some forward thinking school principals and motivated teachers are indeed experimenting with this school-practical work experience concept in Italy too but not on a national level. Meanwhile maths seems to cause a lot of distress and anxiety in 30% of 15-year-olds the OECD found, this figure was even higher in Italy standing at 43%.

What's the new government led by Matteo Renzi going to do about the school system? Upgrading school buildings is a good start but also what goes on inside the schools had to be addressed assessed and effective remedies found fast also to combat stagnating economy, high unemployment and to render Italy more competitive. PM Renzi appointed Stefania Giannini to the post of education minister to find timely, appropriate remedies and the lady minister got down to work like everybody else on Renzi's team. Old, but right, ideas resurfaced, school must have much more autonomy, was one, and the problem of supply teachers on temporary contracts must be resolved, as soon as possible. Giannini proposed to offer permanent jobs to 150,000 teachers by Sep 2015 and hence phase out the system of graduatoria, no more supply teacher on precarious job contracts, in the future concorso will be held to fill in vacant positions and not create a waiting list as now. English, IT, history of art and music will be taught in all schools as early as possible, in the case of English right from primary school. Another revolutionary suggestion was to start teacher assessment and base career advancement, and pay rise, on merit and not only on age and experience. Some put forward the idea of reducing the length of high school by one year, today Italian teenagers are 19 by the time they leave high school, later than in most other countries. In Dec. 2017 the graduatorie were still in place, and some 50,000 supply teachers had to be recruited, just as before, to fill the vacancies.

In an unprecedented move, Renzi's team decided to invite suggestions from Italians on how to improve the school system, a similar consultation had already been carried out by other EU nations like France, Estonia and UK but the response from the Italian public was beyond anyone's expectations, participation was larger than anywhere else. Over two months starting 15 Sep 2014 some 207,000 people put forward ideas online, 1.3 million accessed the website, labuonascuola.gov.it, government set up for the purpose; 130,000 people filled out a questionnaire giving a total of about 6.5 million responses; 5,000 wrote an e-mail outlining their ideas. Who exactly were the participants? Just over half, predictably, were teachers themselves, and 20% parents. Participants suggested that a foreign language (i.e. English) should be taught to reach a much better proficiency than now alongside subjects like music, sport, art, civic education, and more emphasis on psychology and emotional intelligence should be placed. The schools should be open for longer hours (also in the afternoon) and subjects taught should be revised. Teachers should no longer work on temporary contracts with no job security.

There are also private schools in Italy, over 13,600 of them, teaching almost one million kids from 3 to 19 years of age, and charging up to €8,000 per year. Most of these schools are run by religious organisations and by law all pupils attending private schools get part of their tuition paid by the state. In 2014 the state and regional governments paid out nearly €494 million of taxpayers' money to usually middle-class, wealthy families to send their children to privately run schools. In 2015 the amount was cut by a meagre €20 million as part of state spending review. Private schools generally pay less and offer less job security for teachers because there's no shortage of supply teachers who accept low pay to gain points, or credits, to move up the graduatoria and hopefully, eventually, land a permanent post at a state school with better pay and prospects.

What are Italy's high schools like anyway, private or otherwise, certain subjects like Italian and maths are commonly studied in all schools but when it comes to other subjects, the focus changes depending on the type of school. There are six types of high school: Liceo Linguistico (languages), Liceo Scientifico (science); Liceo Classico (Latin, Greek); Liceo Artistico (art);

Liceo delle Scienze Umane (human sciences); Liceo Musicale e Coreutico (music and dance) offering ample choice for all tastes and talents. At the end of high school everyone has to sit an external exam, the dreaded Maturità, and obtain an overall score of 60% to pass calculated by summing written exam results, an oral test and credits obtained at school. Unlike other OECD or EU countries, Italian school system requires teenagers to attend high school till the age of 19; as of 2018, 100 high schools in Italy will adopt a 4-year cycle reducing the age of high school graduation to 18 like everywhere else, if the experiment succeeds, it is expected to apply the shorter cycle to all high schools. Now the lucky 18 or 19-year-old can attend university but which one and how does higher education in Italy work anyway?

FIVE

ITALIAN UNIVERSITIES TODAY

Let's make it clear. Italian university system is in need of urgent reforms too. The Times list of 100 top universities around the world published in Oct. 2008, contained no Italian institutions, Bologna University, the oldest seat of higher learning in Europe (founded 11th century) was placed 192nd (or 78th in Europe), famous La Sapienza of Rome and Bocconi of Milan didn't make the top 200. Come 2013-2014, University of Trento was the highest scoring Italian university, placed 221. On the other hand, just as respectable as The Times rankings, the QS World University Rankings in their 2014 report placed Bologna at 188th, not exactly brilliant but at least it made the top 200 list. Better news came from Financial Times Business Schools Rankings, 2014, regarding Master's in Management. Milan's Bocconi earned 12th place, up 11 places in the preceding two years. Situation has improved in recent years, QS World University Rankings for 2018 included four Italian universities in the top 200: Politecnico of Milan (170th), Bologna University (182nd), Normale of Pisa (192nd) and Superiore Sant'Anna of Pisa (192nd). Whereas, Milan's Bocconi ranked number in Italy but as a specialist university focusing on finance and economics, it was not considered in the general rankings.

Meanwhile OECD poured out revealing statistics on the number of people holding university degrees, in their 2014 report, regarding the year 2012, they found that 22% of Italians aged 25-34 held a university degree occupying the last but one position on the list of 34 countries OECD considered, the OECD average is 40% of graduates. The figures for Italy used to be much worse, in 2000 there were only 11% degree-holders in the 25-34 age group. However, the number of high school graduates applying to universities isn't going up, according to Italy's education ministry during 2003-2004 academic year there were 338,000 undergraduates at Italian universities, 10 years later the number dropped to 226,000, the worrying trend, fortunately, began to point upward, during the 2016 - 2017 the student population rose to around 283,400. The EU objective of 40% of the population having a degree by 2020 is still unlikely to be met, by Italy anyway. Interestingly, a study published in May 2008 by four Italian economists, two lecturing in US universities, the very first parliament of the Republic of Italy (1948-1953) had 91.4% university graduates, the 15th parliament (2006-2008) counted 64.6%. In the same period in the US university graduates in parliament went from 88 to 94%. Today's parliament? About the same as in 2006: 71% graduates in the Camera and 56% in the Senato. The OECD report 2014 highlighted that only 47% of high school leavers go on to university in Italy against 58% average in OECD, some 32% of 20-24 year-olds in 2012 were neets (not in education, employment or training). Italy's neet population decreased by 2017 probably due to economic upturn to around 25% of native Italians but for the immigrant population it stayed the same, around 32%.

Education ministers down the decades have tried to improve the situation. Mariastella Gelmini in 2008 aimed to address the issue just like she did for the schools: by rationalising the entire system, introducing advancement by meritocracy and attracting private funds by allowing state universities to form foundations just like in the US. True enough there is a lot of room for streamlining, there are 94 universities in Italy with estimated 330 branches, over 600 faculties in all, offering an enormous number of courses counting 5,100 in 2007-2008, to some 1.82 million students; over 360 of these courses attracted fewer than 15 students, making them remarkably uneconomical. The increase in the number of courses meant appointing an increasing number of staff, currently there are around 20,000 professors, 19,000 associate professors holding permanent posts and paradoxically only around 23,000 researchers, who, at the bottom of the hierarchy, earn a salary of about €1,350 after three years of experience which is less than half of what the professors make at the beginning of their careers. There are also some 89,000 temporary teaching staff working as assistants, tutors, mother-tongue language teachers etc. The salaries alone absorb on average 90% of the funds.

How did the government address these issues? The state promised to spending €7.5 billion in 2009 but aimed to cut €1.4 billion from the university budgets over the next five years by suppressing uneconomical faculties running uneconomical courses, replacing only half the professors retiring if the university doesn't have a budget deficit; those with a deficit or spend over 90% of their budget on salaries wouldn't be able to appoint new academic staff. This was not as straightforward as it sounds, large scale demonstrations took place across Italy, students protested against these cuts calling them, 'indiscriminate' and voiced worries about 'privatisation' of universities.

In response to protests, Gelmini worked out a more detailed plan with concrete measures. Universities with a good organisation, performing well in scientific research producing top quality graduates would receive €500,000, or 7% of the state funds, that would increase to 30% by 2011. Starting 2009 for every retiring professor two researchers would be employed aiming to give 60% of new posts to researchers. Gifted students would be offered scholarships to the tune of €135 million a year. Italy's public universities are free for the poor but most students pay fees depending on family income, on average fees range from about €500 to €1,400 per year.

Italian universities are often criticised, mostly by the Italians themselves, for nepotism, where an internal commission of professors allegedly appoint not the best candidate but a recommended, local one. Many governments in the past have attempted to prevent this abuse of power by the professors who are referred to as 'baroni,' Gelmini decided to introduce legislation to bring more transparency to the system and to make sure the best applicant gets hired. A pool of professors were hence created nationwide, and every commission was chosen at random from the pool to select the best candidates for university posts. Selection of professors was be made by a commission of five where only one was local, researchers continued to be appointed by a commission of three professors but only one was to be local, and starting 2010 the selection was essentially based on what the candidate had published and on the quality of his dissertation not just the opinion of the professors. Promotion of professors within universities was to depend on academic achievement and to bring back home high profile Italian scientists working abroad, universities were given the power to call them directly and offer posts in Italian institutions. On Jan. 8th, 2009 Gelmini's reform package became law but had to wait till 2010 to be fully applied. "Universities respecting their budget limits, performing well academically will get more funding, we have no more money to waste," commented Gelmini.

Despite bringing in some rationalisation, better rewarding meritocracy, and limiting the power of the 'baroni,' Italian universities haven't improved that much, at least according to Times list and OECD findings mentioned above. Again like the schools, the selection method is the concorso, the admission test, in 2012 around 41,120 researchers and just over 18,000 associate professors sat the test to move up the ladder to become associate professors and ordinary professors respectively. Only some 16,570 researchers and 7,360 or so associate professors managed to pass the test causing cries of foul play, accusations of nepotism, incompetence even corruption of the selection commission, several thousand complained to the ministry and asked for re-assessment of their test scores another 1000 participants took their case to the regional administrative tribunal, well-known with the acronym, TAR, to appeal against their exclusion. For this concorso, the state had already spent €126 million and now has to contend with widespread protests and 1000 court cases.

Until about 10-15 years ago, anyone with a high school diploma could access any university course. Then came 'numero chiuso' (limited places) for some university faculties like the highly popular, medicine. Future doctors had to sit an admission test which is more a general knowledge quiz than medicine-specific. This too came under much criticism, 'why should a medicine candidate know the name of such and such architect that designed such and such building?' Still it remained. In 2014 64,000 high school graduates tried their luck, only 10,550 were deemed bright enough to pursue their dream of becoming a doctor. Predictably, students complained and took their case to TAR, in summer 2014 TAR decided the students were right and 2,000 more of them entered medicine faculties. Giannini, the new education minister, proposed doing away with admission tests starting 2015, saying everyone will be allowed to enrol and they will be assessed at the end of the first year, those with adequate scores will be allowed to continue, just like they do in France.

Important changes have been e introduced in recent years, rather than studying 4-5 years to obtain a degree, undergraduates are given the choice of earning a bachelor's degree after three years called, *Laurea Triennale*, and could then do two more years if they wished and obtain a *Laurea Magistrale* corresponding to a master's degree, only those with this degree could proceed with a PhD degree that would last three years. Regarding investment in R&D, Italy was/is criticised for not spending enough, OECD found that in 2011 Italy spent only 1.25% of its GDP on research, which went up to 1.5% in 2016 but is still much lower than most other OECD nations which averaged 2.4%. With all the reforms taking place this too was addressed by Renzi's team, more investment in R&D was considered a priority but like in other countries private companies, multi-nationals were invited to participate i.e. invest.

Are there any university courses in English in Italy? Yes, in recent years numerous universities across Italy are holding courses in English too having realised that attracting foreign students to study in Italy is even more profitable than tourism. The website universitaly.it lists all the universities that do undergraduate as well as post-graduate courses in English. ISTAT informs that in the academic year 2012 - 2103 there were 67,617 foreign students attending Italian universities, not only in English. Is this a lot? Not compared to UK where 430,000 foreigners from 180 countries attend universities, second placed France attracted nearly 300,000 in 2013, reported Institut Bva Campus France, which generated €1.7 billion of net earnings for the universities and businesses supplying services like transport, food and accommodation. Italian association university graduates, Alma Laurea, announced that 7,431 foreign students graduated from Italian universities in 2013 but as the director of Alma Laurea, Andrea Cammelli put it, "Unlike in other countries, hardly any of these highly trained graduates stay on in Italy, they soon leave taking their useful skills with them." Why that happens is soon explained by the bureaucracy to get a permit to stay and work in Italy and of course the economic recession that hit Italy in recent years reducing job opportunities for all.

Meanwhile, Gelmini reforms are beginning to take effect, new ones by Giannini are bound to improve things further. Italian families are eagerly waiting to see how all these changes are going to affect them. More and more school leavers are looking for a place abroad in UK, Germany and USA mostly, at enormous costs compared to Italy where all universities state run or private get some funding. In the case of medicine by the time a student graduates with a basic medical degree he or she is 25-26 years of age, and if they want to specialise they'll need to study five more years. Just as well Italian families today have very few children, averaging 1.4, next chapter will go into that in more detail.

SIX

ITALIAN FAMILY IN THE 21ST CENTURY

When ISTAT published birth rates in Italy for the year 2016, there was inevitable disappointment, 12,342 fewer babies were born compared to 2015 bringing down the birth rate to 1.35 and if it weren't for babies born to couples with at least one foreign parent, it would have been even lower. According to ISTAT 473,438 babies were born in 2016, the lowest number ever, average age of Italian mothers remained the same, 31.5 years. There are also regional differences, Trentino-Alto Adige had the highest birth rate, 1.65, whereas Liguria with 1.35 had the lowest. How does Italy compare with other European countries? Using Eurostat figures for 2016, in Italy 7.8 babies were born per 1,000 inhabitants, average for the EU was 10 with Ireland leading the table with 13.3 babies, Sweden and UK came second with 11.8 and France third with 11.7 babies. It looks like Italy's population of around 60.5 million today is likely to go down in the long term and not even the immigrant population, standing at around 5.05 million in 2016, is likely to compensate for the diminishing population unless of course more migrants are allowed or invited to come and settle in Italy. Between 2005 and 2014 average birth rates slightly increased from 1.2 to 1.39 but this was thanks to foreign women, unfortunately they have reduced their fertility too, from 2.4 to 1.97. They must have realised bringing a child into the world is one thing bringing it up is another. Raising and educating a child in Italy isn't cheap, according to the findings of consumer organisation, Federconsumatori, from 0 - 18 years of age, on average it costs about the same as a Ferrari California: €171,000 which is 25% more than in 1970s.

Looking after 'children' don't normally stop once they reach the age of 18. More ISTAT figures say nearly seven million under 35-year-olds continue living with the family, that's a staggering 61.2% of total in this group. This also means that they're still single and if remain unmarried 40 even 50-year-olds stay at home, Italian family bonds are truly strong, it's not just a case of economics. Even so the ageing parents are increasingly being looked after by foreign carers originating from places like Eastern Europe and the Philippines. Unless serious measures are taken, Italy is going to get older and older and more and more carers will be needed. In mid-1990s there were 112 aged over 65 for every 100 under 14-year-olds, in 2012 it went up to nearly 149, future projections predict that in 2050 there will be 263 over 65-year-olds for every 100 under 14-year-olds. Meanwhile longevity, fortunately for Italians, keeps going up, in 2016 it was 80.6 years for men and 85.1 for women, that's over seven and nine years more respectively compared to 30 years ago, alas this too is increasing demand for carers.

Are these children born to traditional, married couples? Fewer are these days. Some 28% was born out of wedlock, a substantial rise, back in 2000 the figure was only about 10%. Southern Italians are still defending traditional family, fewer get divorced. ISTAT figures clearly indicate that really is the case, in the north of Italy out of 1,000 marriages 333 end up in divorce, in the south only 180 do. Apparently Naples is one of the few places where marriage rates are actually going up. Across Italy couples in unsuccessful matrimonies opt for separation within three years of living together; paradoxically fewer of southern Italians, under 30%, were married in 2011, that's nearly 7% less than the national average. There are some other unexpected developments regarding the over 65s, they too are untying the knot and going free in increasing numbers. Italy's marriage lawyers' association, Ami (Associazione Avvocati Matrimonialisti Italiani) revealed that 20%

of divorces taking place today involves this mature group, a dramatic increase from the tiny fraction of 2% only 20 years ago.

How easy, and costly, is it to get a divorce in Italy? Bearing in mind till 1974 divorce was illegal, some progress has come about, still it takes more time than most other places. After an official separation, couples have to wait at least three years for a divorce even if it's by mutual consent and if there are children involved or there are disputes to settle it can drag on for years and cost quite a lot. Incidentally as of 2014 there are some five million pending civil cases awaiting a verdict, on average it takes 6-7 years for a case to conclude. Renzi's government wants to speed things up, in straightforward divorce cases with no litigation he's promising a divorce sentence within six months, overall the length of a civil case should be concluded in half the time it's taking now, he said. In this case Renzi kept his promise, Italians can now get divorced within months rather than years. Simplification, speeded up sentencing should also reduce costs dramatically, in the case of divorce by mutual consent it will cost as little as €32 in Piemonte as announced by the local authorities in Turin in Dec 2014 plus perhaps €10 of administration charge. The interested parties began booking a place but they will be summoned and applications processed starting the end of January 2015, the couple will have to then confirm their intention to part ways a month later, and presto they're officially 'separated,' for the actual divorce, and see their marital status changed to 'stato libero' (unmarried) in their ID cards and passports three more years will have to go by, not six months Renzi hoped for. There are other complications on the way, if the couple have underage (under 18) children, or if a child is disabled, this low cost, fast separation/divorce procedure is not applicable.

As a consequence, overall in 21st century Italy 13% of families are of the one-parent type usually one or more children live with the mother and the father pays alimony for their support. How many people live on their own? An analysis of ISTAT figures published in 2017 revealed that as of Jan. 2017, 31.6% of Italians live alone, 20 years ago 20.5% lived on their own. They don't, however, live completely by themselves though, Italians are on the whole pet lovers, despite abandoning tens of thousands of them, dogs in particular, every summer. According to Assalco, Italy's animal welfare association, in 2016 there were about 60 million pets in the country, about the same number as inhabitants, of which about 7 million were dogs, 7.5 million cats, 13 million birds, 30 million fish and 3 million reptiles and small rodents. The single understandably mostly opted for cats, 65% of them own a cat and 22% a dog. Families with children tend to choose dogs more frequently. Meanwhile, only 5.4% of families count five members or more, 20 years ago the figure was 8.1%, in 2016 average Italian had just 2.4 members.

The worrying low birth rates have been tackled by government after government for decades, the best they managed to do was to offer a bonus of up to €1,000, depending on the region of residence, for each baby born. In recent years for low income families €300 for the first six months has been offered to help with nursery and babysitter costs. State-run i.e. free or affordable nurseries and kindergartens are hardly enough, one of the reforms Renzi promised was in fact 'opening a new kindergarten everyday for the next 1,000 days.' Tax benefits for families with children again hardly reduced the costs for having and raising a child, meanwhile birth rates continue stagnating around 1.4. Starting Jan 2015, new legislation took effect to bring in more incentives for families to have children, families earning under €25,000 are to get €960 a year of bonus for three years from the state for each newborn. This generosity took a dive in December 2017 when the amount for 2018 was reduced to just €80 a month and only for the first 12 months of the infant's life.

What names do Italian choose for their newborn? ISTAT informs that in 2016 the top 10 most popular names were:

Boys

1. Francesco

2. Alessandro

3. Leonardo

4. Lorenzo

5. Mattia

6. Andrea

7. Gabriele

8. Matteo

9. Tommaso

10. Riccardo

Girls:

1. Sofia

2. Aurora

3. Giulia

4. Emma

5. Giorgia

6. Martina

7. Alice

8. Greta

9. Ginevra

10. Chiara

These are the names of new generation of Italians but what names are currently most common? More than half are the same as above.

Boys

1. Andrea

2. Luca

3. Marco

4. Francesco

5. Matteo

6. Alessandro

7. Davide

8. Simone

9. Federico

10. Lorenzo

Girls

1. Giulia

2. Chiara

3. Francesca

4. Federica

5. Sara

6. Martina

7. Valentina

8. Alessia

9. Silvia

10. Elisa

Returning to birth rates, there are other ethical issues that have affected Italian demographics in recent decades. Till 1978 abortion and contraception were illegal. Artificial insemination was allowed but not when a donor was involved, in other words an outsider couldn't donate sperm or an ovule to help the couple conceive a child. As they did to abort before 1978, Italians were forced to go abroad to have artificial insemination via a donor at considerable cost. In 2014, Renzi comes on the scene, serious debate on the issue ensues and regional governments are allowed to go ahead with this type of reproduction but have to follow strict guidelines. The skin colour of the donor must be the same as the couple, if a man he must be between 18 and 40 years of age and if a woman between 18 and 35. The mother-to-be can't be over 43. The identity of the donor shall be kept confidential until the child reaches the age of 25 but the donor can choose to remain anonymous even then. Who's going to pay for all this and how much? No easy answer for this one, it will depend on the region one lives in, Emilia-Romagna, central Italy, intends to do it for free, courtesy of Italy's national health service, the others will charge a fee but again the Italian NHS will foot part of the cost, Lombardy region governor Roberto Maroni of Lega Nord party declared this is not a health issue, and the hospitals and clinics offering the service in his region will be charging the full price for it i.e. several thousand euros. Tuscany was the most enthusiastic and was the first to announce they were ready to go ahead in Aug 2014, within days, 200 couples joined the waiting list. Come Oct. waiting lists across Italy had around 1,000 couples eager to take advantage of the service.

Once the child is born, raised and educated as much as possible, he or she will then have to look for a job. Working for an Italian company be it in fashion, engineering, food or drink production will probably give the most satisfaction specially if the product carries the Made in Italy label. What exactly lies behind these three words Italians proudly used as an adjective to mean outstanding, exceptional, excellent...?

SEVEN

MADE IN ITALY

Few nations are more proud of what they make, produce or manufacture than Italy. The threesome, 'Made in Italy,' is used in its English form both by the ordinary citizens and the media as an adjective to indicate supreme quality, good aesthetics and refined taste. At the supermarket Italians scrutinise the labels desperately looking for 'Italy' somewhere be it milk, pasta, cheese, salami, meat, wine, olive oil, fruit, vegetables or anything else you care to mention. It's a word that inspires trust, safety, and value for money. If its fashion we're talking about, then who can equal the likes of Giorgio Armani, Gucci, Prada, Versace etc. etc.? Italians may not be well-known for their engineering skills but they did invent awesome super cars like Bugatti, Lamborghini, Maserati and Ferrari matching engineering, design and enviable marketing skills that have turned these brands, especially Ferrari, into household names at the top of wish lists around the world.

Whether it's food, clothes, textiles, jewellery, accessories or cars, famous, successful brands serving the better-off, the old and new rich around the globe, have kept the demand high for these brands regardless of economic recession, credit crunch or unemployment. When ordinary goods saw a slump in demand, Italy's food and wine exports continued increasing, by 6% in 2013, reaching an all time high of €33 billion, one reason Eataly outlets selling the best of Italian food continues expanding in Italy and opening new stores in major cities in all corners of the world including Dubai, New York, Tokyo and Istanbul.

The fashion business generated around €50 billion in 2012, growing by 4.8% compared to 2011, a small increase was also registered in 2013 and was expected to go up also in 2014 depending on the political situation in Russia hit by EU/USA sanctions that may affect Italy's fashion exports which, worldwide, account just over half of what's produced.

The quintessential example of Italy's famed brands must be the Ferrari. According to the independent, intangible asset valuation consultancy, Brand Finance, Ferrari is currently the most powerful brand anywhere ahead of Coca Cola (2nd), PricewaterhouseCoopers (3rd), Google (5th) and Disney (10th). Italy's leading financial daily, Il Sole 24 Ore, reported that in 2013, Ferrari sold 6,922 cars worldwide, that's 5.4% fewer than in 2012, but generated a record breaking €2.3 billion of business with net profits of €246 million, up by 5.4%. This deliberate reduction in the number of cars sold, paradoxically, or expectedly, resulted in higher profits, after all Ferrari is an exclusive brand and Ferrari makers don't want to inflate the market and undermine its value. Three new models: LaFerrari, Ferrari458 Special and Ferrari California were sold out in no time. Who buys them anyway? 2,035 went to USA, holding the largest market share, followed by China, Hong Kong and Taiwan buying 700 exemplars, in Europe the top importer with 677 cars was UK. Come 2015 Ferrari increased production to 7,664 cars to partly satisfy demand taking care not to inflate the market.

Owning a Ferrari is also an investment it would appear. If the owner can hold on to it long enough, it's bound to become a classic car sooner or later. One particular story printed in New York Times in Feb 2014 is a perfect example. Enzo Ferrari (1898 - 1988) the inventor of the super car had assembled a new model F335S with a 4.1-litre V12 engine to compete in the famed Mille Miglia race. Alas, in 1958 the rules changed, The World Sports Car Championship only allowed cars up to 3.0-L engines. Enzo was desperately looking for funds to build a racing car, hence badly needed the revenue for the sale of cars like F335S which were really only slightly different from racing cars. He looked to America as the only place to sell his cars. One such final exemplar was bought by a Texan named Alan Connell who used it in races in 1958 and 1959 but realised the engine began performing poorly. The car was sent back to Italy for repairs and came back with a hefty bill of $70,000, Connell refused to retrieve it arguing a new Ferrari cost $12,000. Ferrari 335S languished in US Customs warehouse in New York till 1963 when Gordon Tatum, a Maryland car dealer, noticed it paid the storage fee of $1,000 and took it home. It was sold to Ferrari vintage car enthusiasts in Britain, Japan and finally in Seattle, USA in 1990s before being sold in a private transaction to an Austrian collector, Andreas Mohringer for $21.5 million at the end of 2013. This however was not the highest price ever paid for a vintage car, the record was held by a 1954-model Mercedes-Benz W196 sold for $29.7 million in summer 2013 in Chichester, England. In Aug 2014 all that changed, a Ferrari 250 GTO Berlinetta made in 1962 fetched a record breaking $38.1 million at Bonhams Quail Lodge Auction in Carmel, California. In comparison brand new Ferraris cost peanuts, 2014-models: Ferrari California, Ferrari 458, and Ferrari Berlinetta can be had starting around €187,000; €206,000; and €277,000 respectively.

    Ferrari is also a tourist attraction, there are two museums, one in Modena, the birthplace of Enzo Ferrari, known as Museo Casa Enzo Ferrari, this is where the great, passionate car engineer lived, and another at Maranello, nearby, where Ferrari factory is based. Casa Museo was restored, expanded and inaugurated in Mar 2014 and is bound to draw many Ferrari fans like the one in Maranello which attracts some 322,000 visitors a year. Needless to say both museums display new and vintage Ferrari models as well as memorabilia concerning Enzo Ferrari.

    Besides the big names in fashion, food, wine and cars, there are small, usually family-run concerns, that produce sought-after handicraft up and down Italy. Currently around 1.34 million firms of artisans making up around 24% of total companies in Italy are busy creating top quality, hand-made products that range from beautiful ceramics in Sicily, Faenza and Deruta (Umbria) to leatherwear in Florence, cashmere sweaters in Prato and Viareggio (both in Tuscany), marble sculptures in Carrara, shirts and tailor-made suits in Naples, church bells in Molise, violins in Cremona, glass artworks in Murano, unique womenswear in Milan, silk accessories in Como, made to measure shoes in Varese, furniture in Brianza (Lombardy), jewellery in Valenza (Piemonte) and much, much more. Yet some 75,000 of these artisan firms closed down over the five years, 2008-2013 due to economic crisis but not only that, craftwork is not attracting the young generations who do not apparently want to do manual work, however skilled however in demand. Artisan association of Mestre, Cgia, calculated that by 2020 some 385,000 artisan jobs in carpentry, upholstery and embroidery, for instance, will remain vacant, prompting Italian firms seriously to look for immigrant workforce to fill the gap.

Italy's famous brands have been attracting much interest in the world of high finance and investment over the last decade or so, according to Il Sole 24 Ore some 500 brands have been sold to foreigners. The long list includes Lamborghini that now belongs to Germany's VW, Krizia and Riso Scotti are Chinese, Valentino belongs to an emir in Qatar, Fiorucci is Spanish, Fendi, Bulgari, Gucci, Pucci, Acqua di Parma, Bottega Veneta are French, Frau, Buitoni, Perugina, Pernogotti, Amaro Avena, San Pellelgrino, Birra Peroni and Parmalat are American, FIAT has transformed into FCA (Fiat Chrysler Automobiles), and 49% of Alitalia is now the property of Qatar's Etihad. When in Sep 2014, the president of Ferrari, Luca Cordero di Montezemolo, was replaced by Sergio Marchionne, the CEO of FCA that owns Ferrari and Maserati, rumours soon spread that Ferrari would become American, Marchionne quickly reassured that Ferrari would always be Italian, and made in Italy otherwise it wouldn't be Ferrari.

More Italian brands are likely to be sold off to, or taken over by, non-Italian business and investment groups in the coming years. A report by, Il Sole 24 Ore, published mid-Nov, 2014, quoting the results of international research group, Icm, informed that the top 10 Italian brands, ranked by market value, foreign groups will probably seek to control are:

1. Liu Jo - fashion house
2. Canali - fashion house
3. Roberto Cavalli - fashion house
4. Furla - fashion leatherwear
5. Pasta Divella
6. Capri - fashion house
7. Imap Export (owners of Original Marines brand)
8. Mutti - tomato products
9. Molteni - furniture
10. iGuzzini - lighting

They are reportedly worth between €112 million (Liu Jo) and €58 million (iGuzzini).

Italians are naturally proud of their brands and there's outcry every time a foreign firm or multinational steps in and takes over a well-known make but what really infuriates the whole nation is the illegal or otherwise imitation of Italian products all over the world. An estimate made by Coldiretti, the 1.5-million-member-strong association of Italian agriculture-related businesses, fake Italian products generate €60 billion worth of trade worldwide to the detriment of authentic products which earn the Italian producers some €37 billion in 2016, much less than the fakes. The most imitated seems to be Parmesan cheese that can easily be encountered in USA, Canada, Australia and Japan; similar-sounding names abound like Parmesao in Brazil, Regianito in Argentina (Parmesan is known as Parmigiano-Reggiano in Italy) or Reggiano e Parmesao all over South America, and Pamesello in Belgium. In UK, USA and Australia you can buy a kit and make your own 'authentic' Parmesan. You can also buy a kit and make Valpolicella wine. How about Canadian made Pecorino Friulano or Crotonese Cheese, German-made Gorgonzola Sauce and Prosciutto Cotto Villa Gusto, Romanian Mortadella Siciliana, Brasilian Milano Salami? The list is long but here are some more gems: German Maccaroni Mit Tomatensauce and Gnocchi Rucola-Parmesan; Pompeian Olive Oil in Maryland, USA, fake Chianti also in USA, and Prosecco imitations like Kresecco and Meer-Secco again in Germany; there's even a Romanian Barbera whereby the famously red wine turns white in the Romanian version.

Italian government has been protesting against this unethical, illegal imitation and been putting pressure on the World Trade Organisation to put an end to this by making it compulsory to clearly indicate the origin of the product, alas it is not even being done in the EU where an olive oil label for instance only says it was made by olives from EU nations (Greece, Italy, Cyprus, Spain) without specifying which.

Imitation is one thing, passing off a counterfeit brand for authentic is even worse, yet this is so widely practised that it would probably be impossible to eliminate. China, Turkey, Thailand for instance quite openly make counterfeit Italian labels, among others, which are not only sold in the country of origin but are also exported, huge quantities also turn up in Italy, frequently Italian customs discover containers-full of merchandise or lorry-full of designer items. There are websites people can order fake Hogan shoes from China. The argument goes that those buying know what they're buying is fake, they're buying designer items on the cheap and are fully aware of this. One reason in places like Turkey and Thailand this practice is tolerated by the local authorities.

Paradoxically a huge quantity of designer labels are also illegally produced in Italy itself. In Aug 2014 Italy's financial police confiscated 120,000 fake designer bags and shoes bearing Made in Italy labels in Naples and its surrounds. Made in Italy they were, ironically, but illegally and hardly lived up to the quality of the originals. According to newspaper reports, organised crime syndicates using illegal immigrants as vendors sold the bags and shoes on Italy's beaches and tourist haunts. In 2013 this illegal trade in Italy generated a massive €1.5 billion on the black market, it was estimated.

Talking of luxury and designer items, I'd really like to tell you what's happening in Como, my adopted home, where some of Italy's most sought-after designer silk accessories, and fabrics, are created. Quality silk manufacturing in Como has been going on since 16th century, you can read the full story in the next chapter.

EIGHT

SILK ARTWORKS OF COMO

"Half the merit goes to a domesticated, blind butterfly scientists call, Bombyx Mori," said Signor Masciadri, the curator of the Museum of Silk in Como, "without it we wouldn't have silk, the illustrious raw material used in Como to create works of art. Did you know that the tie Bill Clinton wore on the day he was elected president came from Como?"
"I had no idea," I said.
"Probably Clinton, [and ensuing presidents, Bush, Obama and Trump] was in good company, many of the high-fashion silk accessories and sensuously rustling clothes worn at his victory celebrations, most likely originated in Como too."
"I had no idea," I said again but thinking about it, Italian silk accessories bearing well-known designer signatures are probably worn at any high-ranking occasion including the victory celebrations of ensuing US presidents, Bush, Obama and Trump.

      The museum is part of an establishment aptly named, Setificio (silk-factory), which educates and trains Como's silk artisans of the future. The curator proudly took me from room to room explaining how silk fabrics are born, from the cultivation of silkworms, harvesting of the cocoons to weaving of the threads to dyeing and printing. Ample space is devoted to the history of silk manufacturing in the city. On display are 19th and early 20th-century handlooms, rudimentary machines and tools for reeling, dyeing and printing of the woven fabrics. On entering a laboratory set up inside the museum, Masciadri explained how the dyes were weighed, mixed and concentrated in the old days.

      Como identifies itself with silk at its best. Numerous fashion designers around the globe commission silk from Como that has made the city famous worldwide and brought much pride, and wealth, to the townspeople. At its peak, up to the year 2000, the city and its environs had some 2,400 highly specialized firms involved in the silk or other textile industries employing some 40,000 people. South-East Asian competition, Chinese in particular, meant the number of firms declined to 800 over the next 15 years of so but quality silk production is still going on. Excepting the large companies like Ratti and Mantero, who have their own textile designers, weaving, dyeing and printing factories, increasingly the others now deal with just one of the stages that will lead to the expensive, silk artworks. The total number of printers for instance went down from 200 to 60 over the last 10 years or so.

      Even so, silk and other textiles, generated around €2.1 billion in 2001, a decade or so later €2.5 billion was generated, over half of which from exports. Como's silk makers restructured, streamlined and innovated to compete with Asian companies that can produce with much cheaper labour. Ratti was taken over by Marzotto, Mantero reduced its workforce from 1,000 in the year 2000 to around 450 in 2016 but reporting profits of €78 million for 2015 the firm began hiring again and expected to increase profits by further 10% over the following year. Firms have also become highly flexible, they can produce limited amounts of fabrics for niche markets, focus is on quality, creativity, sustainability and professional work ethics e.g. delivery on time resulting in maintenance of acceptable profit margins. Technology is giving a hand too, whereas before nearly everything was done by hand, now the designs are transferred to a digital file and printing automated, helping save time, energy and costs. But digital technology has its pitfalls too, it's easy to copy, anyone with the file in their hands can go into production anytime, anywhere.

      In recent years there has also been a shift towards more ecological, sustainable methods, firms like La Canepa which employs 700, has been collaborating with Milan's Politecnico (university) to find more environment friendly methods to produce textiles; their investment has produced results, now less water and energy is necessary to manufacture the same quantity of textiles and even more importantly 30-40% less chemicals are used for dyeing; they are aiming to reduce polluting chemicals by 75% in the near future. A natural substance known as, chitin, abundant in the exoskeletons of crustaceans and insects was discovered in France in 1821, it is now being used in Como in textile production as an alternative to chemical polymers. The cellulose-like chitin helps produce fine textiles and is much easier to manage as a waste product.

How is a silk artwork created anyway? Masciadri in his soothing voice began at the beginning. "As I said, the merit goes to Bombyx Mori which lays the eggs that produce the silkworms" he said, "although there are some 500 wild varieties of caterpillars that can produce silk fibres, the Bombyx is the most widely used because compared to the wild varieties the protein-rich filament it ejects is more regular, smoother and rounder hence it doesn't break or entangle; it absorbs dyes better, and is so resistant that one cocoon can yield a continuous strand of up to 1 km long, weight per weight it is stronger than steel. Before the silkworm in its pupa stage has a chance to release an enzyme to break the cocoon it has built around itself and leave as a butterfly, the cocoons are subjected to steam or hot air to kill off the larva and interrupt the cycle. They are then washed in soap and water to get rid of the gummy substance that wraps around the fibres. Several filaments, depending on the thickness required, are then put together to render the threads robust enough for weaving, dyeing and printing."

As soon as I left the museum, new questions arose in my head. What makes silk so shiny, how many cocoons are needed to make a tie or a blouse? How many silkworms does it take to produce a kg of silk? Are the threads dyed before the weaving process or after? Who is behind the motives printed on the fabrics?

I quizzed Matteo Mottin, a Setificio graduate with a decade of experience in silk production, "Silk fibres are triangular," he responded, "and reflect light just like a prism giving silk its luxurious sheen and feel, it takes about 100-120 cocoons to make a tie, six times as many will be necessary for a blouse. More than 5,000 silkworms will be needed to produce about 1 kg of raw silk. For quality, threads should be dyed before weaving but not always. The crinkly crepe fabrics are woven first and dyed second for best results. Some fabrics like twill have equal number of warp (vertical) and weft (horizontal) fibres and are ideal for printing, others such as satin has more warp than weft, is shiny and unsuitable for printing hence you would rarely find printed satin." To find out what is printed on the fabrics and who creates them Mottin advised me to contact some textile artists/designers in Como.

  I did. Not difficult bearing in mind the city harbours many studios which do nothing but create new motifs and patterns usually the traditional way, by hand, but computers are being more and more frequently used too. I found the field fiercely competitive and surprisingly cosmopolitan. I spoke to Ikuko Fujii, a Japanese designer based in Como, she recounted, "designing is like writing, you sit facing a blank piece of paper, or silk in my case, and try to create something different, but not too different, after all people will wear these things. A lot of research goes into what's trendy, we get some input from specialized magazines or from our clients or agents in various countries, but these rarely go beyond suggestions like 'exotic,' 'metallic,' 'floral' or 'hippy' you then literally let your imagination go wild, but not too wild." "After all people will wear these things" I said jokingly, "Exactly" she nodded several times.

  Alessandra Guffanti, a designer from Como, echoed much the same content and added, "sometimes a client may turn up with a pattern scrawled on a scrap of paper, or a magazine cutting and explain to us what he or she has in mind. We then have to create a brand new design to make his or her dreams come true. If it's a tie, it might take an entire day to get it right, for a foulard around 10 days will be necessary."

Can't computers help? I put the question to Sergio Castelli who utilizes computer aided design (CAD), "computer is but an aid, just as A in CAD implies" he said, "it helps you to make complex geometric patterns, variants, or you can scan and elaborate hand-made designs, try out numerous backgrounds for instance, and do it all very quickly. But in the case of foulard, it's very hard for a computer to reproduce the type of detail the human hand, and brain, can achieve."

"Do you only design for silk ?"

"No. What comes out of studios in Como are also printed on other types of textiles. But most of it will end up in the Alta Moda (high fashion) or Prêt-à-Porter (ready to wear) niches. The client chooses what appeals most and the whole process of accessory, dressmaking or upholstery manufacturing is thus initiated.

How much would a silk accessory Made in Como cost? I put the question to Signor Hellali, a sales executive for a number of Italian brands such as Mantero, Ferré, Ungaro, Trussardi, DKNY and Kenzo. "A tie with these brands will come to €70-90. Others such as Bulgari or Naples-based Kiton can charge up to €120" he said. "Don't the clients ever ask for specific designs?" "Yes, a lot of collaboration takes place. Some like Ferré presents us a motive on paper and we transform that onto fabric, others generate ideas from something that's inspired them, our designers match, try to match, what's required, eventually when the right images, colours, texture, finish is decided upon we go into production." Over at Ratti there are other illustrious names like Versace, Gucci, Dolce & Gabbana and Christian Dior queuing up for the company's accessories and fabrics. A foulard carrying one of these signatures is no less than a work of art and can fetch €200-€300. That's of course cheap considering a dress can cost €2,000-€3,000. Both Mantero and Ratti as well as numerous other silk companies in Como also produce their own brands signed by Italian but unimpressive names. But they are also Made in Como just like Versace, Gucci, Ferrè et al, how come they cost a third to a half. Hellali smiled, " Often the fabrics used for designer items are of superior quality but that's not the whole story. If you see two paintings of equal beauty with the same price tag but one is signed Cézanne and the other, say, Hellali, which would you purchase?" Point taken.

Although the origin of silk is veiled in mystery, it is generally agreed that it was first woven in China millennia ago. Traditionally it was Hsi-ling-shi, the wife of the legendary emperor Huang-ti, who discovered silk around mid-3rd millennium BC. Apparently a cocoon fell into her hot tea and revealed the lustrous filaments to her. More concrete evidence came in the form of red fragments of textile discovered in the township of Qianshanyang in the Chinese province of Zhejiang and carbon dated to 3,000 BC making it the oldest known silk fabric anywhere. In the same area, close to the town of Wu-hsing, more silk strands were excavated which dated back to 2850-2650 BC. Close inspection indicated that the raw material was supplied by none other than Bombyx Mori!

During the era of the Shang Dynasty (founded 1760-1520 BC, ended 1122-1030 BC), the first Chinese dynasty to enjoy both archaeological and written records, that commerce moved westwards, but was still a long way from Europe. When the Silk Road was officially inaugurated in early 2nd century BC, silk goods made their way across Central Asia to the port town of Antioch (Eastern Turkey) and via the sea they triumphantly entered Rome. At the court of Julius Caesar, the wealthy, noble and powerful revelled in its luxury. Silk was literally worth its weight in gold in Rome.

Despite its presence throughout the Roman Empire from Rome to Constantinople (Istanbul), the Chinese guarded the secret of sericulture so well that nobody had any idea how to produce silk in the West. The illustrious scholar, naturalist Pliny the Elder, a native of Como, believed silk was, "hair of sea-sheep." Others thought it was fleece that grew on trees or that it came from the bark of a shrub. Byzantine Emperor Justinian I (527-565 AD) under pressure for enormous demand for silk adopted a devious method to obtain the know-how to produce the lustrous fibre locally. He persuaded Persian monks to smuggle Bombyx Mori silkworm eggs and mulberry seeds into Constantinople around 550 AD hence prompting silk production there.

Once the dominance of Constantinople faded around 9th-century, cities in Syria and Greece took over. The Moors introduced sericulture to Spain and later to Sicily in the 11th-century. Improved silk production skills flowered in the Tuscan city of Lucca in the 13th century and an organization of producers that went by the name of L'Arte della Seat (art of silk) was set up. It was the artisans of Lucca that invented velvets in 1300s. With the demise of the city-state of Lucca at the hands of Pisa, the art of silk moved to Florence and then to Venice early 15th century.

As Renaissance got underway in Tuscany, sericulture took hold in the Dukedom of Milan to which Como belonged. As the power of Milan's dukes, the Visconti, declined, silk production increasingly seeped into Lake Como area, indeed the first silk-spinning factory was set up at the pretty, lake-side village of Bellano in 1510, by 1550s the villagers were producing silk drapes. In 1599 Prince Frederick, the Duke of Wuttenberg, Germany, visiting Lake Como noted, "On both sides of the lake are mountains and villages. The region produces much wine, abounds in chestnuts, olive and mulberry trees; it also produces much silk." According to Milan's city archives, in mid-16th century Como had 124 silk mills, twice as many was recorded in 1748, one in seven of the city's 14,000 inhabitants worked in the silk industry. Around 1840 the countryside of Lake Como was draped by three million mulberry trees whose leaves supply the only food the silkworms feed on. The city's reputation as a supplier of quality silk permeated more and more markets at home and abroad. Fashion designers in the 20th century had no difficulty when they looked for top class silk and Como's silk artworks went from strength to strength.

Today around 20,000 people are employed in Como's silk industry. Smart shops and many factory stores in and around Como proudly display what is currently on offer. The silk artworks in these establishments are as much a tourist attraction as are the pretty, Nordic sceneries of Lake Como.

Despite the abundance of silk in Como, today not a strand comes from cocoons cultivated locally. Labour costs being what they are, all the raw silk is imported from China, the major supplier all over the world. It's as if the Bombyx Mori 1,500 years after it was smuggled into the West via Istanbul, has flown back home to China. Even so Como hasn't entirely given up on silk production, some companies such as Mantero have started up joint-venture enterprises with Chinese partners and are directly involved in silk production. Once raw silk yarns or woven fabrics reach Como, they are processed and metamorphosed into fabulous accessories, garments or upholstery causing a vertiginous increase in the price of finished products along the way. Wealthy Chinese paradoxically have become the new clients of designer silk accessories made in Italy, mostly in Como

In 1997 American customs decided it was inaccurate to label Como's silk foulards, Made in Italy, because the transformation of the raw materials was not by customs' definition 'substantial' to merit this label, instead Made in China should, they argued, replace it or clearly state that the item was only woven, dyed, printed and finished in Italy. Ties on the other hand were deemed sufficiently transformed to be tagged, Made in Italy. Italians naturally appealed to the WTO (World Trade Organization), arguing that it was like importing wood from Norway, making an excellent violin out of it and then having to label it, Made in Norway. US customs remained unimpressed.

They sent inspectors to Como to verify. Once they saw what Como's silk artisans at Mantero, Ratti, Canepa, Clerici, etc. do to dull-looking raw silk strands, the inspectors decided the wood-violin analogy was accurate after all. Como's sophisticated silk products regained their Made in Italy appellation.

Although sericulture as a way of life in Como has disappeared, a new culture which concentrates on transforming raw silk into artworks has taken its place. As Masciadri put it "Silk is a symbol, an identity, and a lifeline for our city. It is silk, as well as the beauty of our lake, that put us on the map. We have to not only cherish but also protect our silk heritage."

Creating a brand, a lovingly manufactured piece, is one thing, turning something that nature offers into a most-desired product is something else. That's exactly what's happened with truffles, especially white truffles, that Italy exports; another is the fine chocolate, unbeknownst to many, Italians make excellent chocolate both for refined gourmets and the masses, does Nutella ring a bell? Unlike truffles that are skilfully gathered in Italy's woods, cacao has to be imported from faraway places like South America or Africa and transformed into a sought-after brand, much like silk. Next chapter is entirely devoted to truffles and chocolate.

NINE

TRUFFLES AND CHOCOLATE

The village of Acqualagna counting 4,300 inhabitants is but 25 km from the hugely famous city of Urbino in Le Marche region of central Italy but Acqualagna, though not that distinguished for its history or monuments, is hugely famous for the quality and quantity of truffles it produces. Some 50 - 60 tons of white (tuber magnatum pico), black (tuber melanosporum), bianchetto (tuber borchii) and summer black (tuber aestivum) change hands every year in Acqualagna amounting to some two thirds of the entire Italian truffle production.

Giorgio Remedia, an experienced *tartufaio* (truffle gatherer) explains to me that "Today truffle harvesting is no longer the tartufaio setting out early in the morning if not in the dead of night to roam the woods to find prized exemplars in secret corners away from the prying eyes of competitors. Some 100 tartufai in Acqualagna now mostly own their truffle wood, ours measures some 80 hectares, and like me and my father, now aged 80, go truffle hunting whenever they feel like it. You may collect as much as 500g to a kilo a day."

Can you actually cultivate truffles? Remedia responds,"White truffles (the most expensive) have not been successfully farmed, but other types of truffles can be farmed by re-creating the ideal conditions where truffles in the wild grow, for instance by clearing land in a wooded area like ours, planting trees like Roverella (a type of oak) and grafting their roots with truffles; it might take 8 - 10 years before you see any fruits, but it works." Starting 1982 Le Marche region has been restoring woods and promoting truffle farming in the area. This way they hope to provide the younger generations with job opportunities and prevent depopulation of rural townships.

Acqualagna may hold the record for the overall quantity but when it comes to individual size it was outdone by a lump of 1.5 kg of white truffle unearthed in the woods of Palaia, a town near Pisa, in 2007, by a father and son team, Luciano and Cristiano Savini; it was the largest of its kind to be found till then, the Pisa truffle soon hit the world media, a satellite auction was organised and eventually Stanley Ho, a Macao casino-owner, purchased it by offering a record $330,000 outbidding sultan Mansoor Bin Sayeed Al Nahyan of Dubai by $10,000. The speedy sale of a white truffle is a must, the tuber must be consumed within 20 days of its discovery otherwise it loses its legendary pungent, garlicky aroma. Truffle auctions are also held in the Grinzane Cavour castle, near Turin, and the recently opened truffle museum in the Tuscan village, San Giovanni d'Asso, near Siena. The proceeds go to a charity organisation. In 2008 at Grinzane Cavour, the largest 'lump' weighing 750g was sold for €100,000 to Crown Wine Cellars of Hong Kong. A total of €250,000 was collected at this by now famous charity truffle auction attended by international celebrities that reached its 14th edition in 2013 when even more money was raised by the sale of 11 lots for a total of €274,000. Two largest pieces weighing a handsome 950 grams were purchased by a Chinese lady, apparently a writer, who dished out €90,000 but chose to remain anonymous, another buyer was a businessman who bought a 305-gram 'gem' and was intent to offer it to Bill De Blasio, the mayor of New York. Come Nov, 2014, a piece of sensational truffle news captured culinary headlines around the world, a huge lump of white truffle weighing an all time record of, 1.89 kg (4.16 lb) had just been unearthed by 32-year-old Matteo Casadei, of Ravenna, and his dog, Ray. Offers of €1 million soon arrived from Dubai and China but the generous tartufaio and family decided to have the awesome lump auctioned in New York and donate the proceeds to charity. The annual auction at Grinzane, now with simultaneous satellite connection with Hong Kong and Dubai, is still going on, in 2017 the proceeds totalled yet another record of €370,000.

Bruno Campana, the mayor of Acqualgna insists truffles are not only good to eat, they have aphrodisiac properties, and supports his claim scientifically, "truffles contain a substance, androstenol, that mimics the action of testosterone," he explains. Other notables past and present have drawn inspiration from truffles. Poet Lord Byron kept a lump on his desk insisting it helped him be creative, author Alexandre Dumas took refuge in it, he defined it a sancta sanctorum, a sanctuary, designer Tom Ford added black truffle to a new perfume he created in 2006 as a prime note. But truffles don't come cheap, the whites can fetch €1,000 - €3,000 a kilo whereas the cheapest varieties are no less than €300 a kilo. Le Langhe area with Alba as capital, in Piedmont, produces most of the other third of Italian truffles. The whites of Piedmont are slightly different (tuber magnatum), they have a more intense aroma and fetch even more, in recent years the prices have shot up as high as €6,000 a kilo. For the latest truffle-bourse info it's best to check out, www.acqualagna.com www.fieradeltartufo.org

But what is a truffle exactly? It is an underground version of spore-containing fungus like mushrooms that grow overground. They live in symbiosis with the roots of trees like oak, beech, hazel, willow and poplar. They have adapted to severe weather conditions like droughts, fires and cold by going underground to survive. The first mention of truffles appears in the writings of Greek philosopher/naturalist Theophrastus (372 – 287 BC), the successor of Aristotle. First century AD Roman scholar Pliny the Elder defined truffles, "One of those things that are born but can't be sown." Romans used truffles in their cuisine but not the prized white and black ones, they opted for the pale, rose tinged, terfezia (terfezia bouderi), aka desert truffle, an odourless variety which was used more like a spice; terfezia truffles absorbed flavour surrounding them and enriched the dish. Historically terfezia was the main truffle variety used all over the Middle-East. Italian traveller Ludovico di Varthema who spent six years travelling across the Middle-East, in his book, Travels (1503-08), noted that great quantities of terfezia harvested in the mountains of Turkey and Armenia were being traded. After keeping a low profile for centuries prized truffles made an appearance at the court of French king, Francis I in 16th century, it took another century before Western cuisine began truly appreciating the natural flavours in their food in place of oriental spices. In late 1700s Paris markets imported ever popular seasonal truffles including by then famed whites from Italy, then as now they were expensive and enjoyed mainly by the noble and the rich. Since then truffle fans have multiplied no end and the entire production of Italian truffles for example are snapped up within weeks of being unearthed.

How does one go looking for truffles. Signor Remedia explains, "You must have a trained dog like our bloodhound, Lola, or a cross between a bloodhound and pointer or even a lagotto (water dog). But other types of dogs can also be trained to hunt truffles."Acqualagna today trains some 70% of Italian truffle dogs. The sows may have been the first discoverers of truffles drawn by the odour of androstenol the tuber contains.

What do you do with truffles? Needless to say given the price they're used sparingly, white truffles are usually served raw shaved over steaming pasta or risotto as well as cold dishes like salads.

Both white and black are also used in pates, stuffing, roasted meat or even with some cheeses. Black truffles have a less intense, subtler aroma similar to mushrooms. Truffle lovers today as in the past don't mind paying the price for it or weep over it as musician Gioachino Rossini did, "I have wept three times in my life. Once when my first opera failed. Once again when I heard Paganini play the violin. And the third time when truffled turkey went overboard at a boating picnic."

Truffle gathering is an all-year activity in Acqualagna, three main truffle events are held :

Fiera Nazional del Tartufo Bianco - Oct - Nov - the most important white truffle fair attended every year by over 100,000 people.

Fiera Regionale del Tartufo Nero Pregiato – prized black truffle fair held third week in Feb.

Fiera Regionale del Tartufo Nero Estivo – summer black truffle fair held first weekend in Aug.

Fiera d'Alba – the main Piedmont white truffle fair has been held since 1929 every Oct -Nov in Alba.

You can blend chocolate with truffles and have the best of both worlds. Truffles and chocolate in a variety of combinations, mostly in desserts or sweet snacks, are indeed available in Italy and elsewhere. But let's take a look at the world of Italian chocolate which really is full of surprises. "What people passionate about chocolate have in common is not a dependence but a love for chocolate," says   Denis Buosi, an artisan chocolate maker based in Varese, Northern Italy. "I was trained as a pastry chef but 20 years ago I realised what a fantastic raw material chocolate was, so malleable, soft and delicious. You can go beyond the chocolate bars and pralines and create new shapes, blend aesthetics and taste." Buosi has won awards at chocolate events in Vienna, Berlin and Italy. By studying ancient cookery books he came up with 'buosino,' an espresso chocolate blend.

Buosi is but one of some 450 registered artisan chocolate makers across Italy who have turned chocolate making into an art form. Italy's chocolate industry makes around €3.2 billion annually but of this €350 million is generated by artisans. What exactly distinguishes artisan made chocolate? Buosi points out close control of stages from the bean to the final product, avoidance of preservatives or other additives detrimental to quality, natural flavourings only, and respecting the environment. Cecilia Tessieri, running Amedei based in Pontedera, Tuscany, with her brother and staff of 25, gives more details, "We own two cacao plantations in Venezuela to have full control of cocoa beans. My brother Alessio also roams Ecuador, Trinidad, Madagascar and Jamaica searching for excellent quality, he sends me samples to Italy to test, if all goes well, he goes ahead with the purchase. Then there's the creative aspect, the art of creating new taste. Chocolate has many forms it can be solid, liquid, powder or granular, blending it in the right proportions with the right ingredients is an act of creation but at the base of it all is the quality of the raw materials." This near-obsessive attention to quality has paid off, in very recent years the Amedei took home three Golden Bean prizes awarded by London Chocolate Academy in the dark chocolate category. In Tuscany spread in the triangle between Florence, Pisa and Pistoia, there are many other chocolatiers and artisans like the firms Pistocchi and Stainer, in all around 50 small centres each employing half a dozen workers on average produce delicious chocolate bars and hand decorated pralines that are exported all over the world.

Although chocolate is not the first thing that springs to mind where Italian food is concerned, it's been a part of Italian culinary tradition for a long time. Officially Italy's Cristoforo Colombo (Christopher Columbus) was the first European to see cocoa beans, he tasted them but wasn't keen on the bitter taste. He took samples to his employers Isabelle and Ferdinand of Spain in 1502 but the first shipload of cocoa beans sailed to Spain from south America only in 1585. Wealthy Spaniards were the first to enjoy chocolate but only as a sweetened drink. Cocoa beans were introduced to Italy by a Tuscan businessman called, Francesco D'Antonio Carletti, as early as 1606. The first chocolate house opened shop in London in 1657 and Maria Teresa of Spain introduced hot chocolate to France when she went to Paris to marry Louis XIV in 1660. National library of Florence keeps many historical documents relating to Italy's chocolate culture narrating of Tuscan nobles who met and downed hot chocolate in large quantities; there's for instance a detailed recipe by Francesco Reti, physician of Duke Cosimo Medici III (1642-1723), who prescribed hot chocolate flavoured with jasmine and cinnamon to help the duke with his digestion.

The next big thing regarding chocolate consumption came in the early decades of 19th-century when the first moves were made to produce chocolate in large quantities and in solid form. Here too, Italians were deeply involved. Caffarel of Turin employed a water-powered machine to grind the cacao beans and blend the resulting powder with vanilla, another similar machine could produce some 320 kilos of chocolate a day in 1826, a record for its time. In 1815 François-Louis Cailler of Switzerland came to work at Caffarel where he learnt the art of making chocolate, after four years of apprenticeship he returned to his hometown of Corsier, near Vevey, to start the first chocolate factory in Switzerland in 1819. Caffarel is but one of some 30 chocolate makers in the Piemonte region with Turin as its capital. Some of the best known brands, Ferrero Rocher and Novi are based here, so are some of the oldest such as Stratta operating since 1836 or the refined Peyrano. During Napoleonic wars the price of cacao rose sharply, Caffarel and other Piemontese chocolate makers decided to use powdered hazel nuts to reduce the need for cacao, hence was born a new flavour which led to the invention of Gianduiotto, the best known chocolate to come out of Piemonte. The famed Baci Perugina pralines made in the Umbrian city of Perugia is another good example of Giandiuotto which as an added bonus each praline contains a whole hazelnut.

Chocolate bars as we know them had to wait till 1847 when Joseph Fry of Bristol, UK, managed to separate cocoa butter from cocoa powder and blend them into a paste without adding water, solid chocolate was thus born. Meanwhile the Swiss introduced further refinements like the mixing machine, mélangeur, invented by Philippe Suchard, to do the hard work of blending the cacao paste and sugar evenly. In 1879 Rudolfe Lindt went a step further by coming up with the conching machine whereby smooth, shiny, creamy chocolate can be obtained. The same year Henri Nestlé discovered a method to obtain powdered milk and teamed up with chocolate maker Daniel Peter to make milk chocolate for the first time.

Interest in chocolate especially dark chocolate products made by artisans has grown considerably in recent years and Italian producers are increasingly focusing on top quality to fight back competition as they do in other fields like fashion and high-performance cars such as Ferrari and Maserati. It was also helped by studies carried out in Italy, Scotland, Switzerland as well as US that dark chocolate which contains high levels of flavonoids, substances known to have an anti-oxidant effects, is good for our health. Blood flow was reported to improve, American Heart Association found that a few chunks of dark chocolate a day had blood-thinning, clot-breaking effect like aspirin and could almost halve the risk of a heart attack. Meanwhile, numerous chocolate events are organised up and down Italy every year. The best attended, Florence (late Jan.), Turin (Mar.), Modica in Sicily (Mar.), Bologna (Nov.) and Perugia (Oct.) attract 100s of 1000s each to their open-air chocolate fairs that last up to 10 days.

Chocolate consumption, however, has its ups and downs. In summer few people think much about eating chocolate especially in warm countries. In summer months many famous brands disappear from the shelves. One reason Northern Europeans and others living in cool/cold climes eat much more chocolate than Italians themselves, the Swiss top the table with around 12 kilos a head, the British get through more than nine kilos and Italians under four kilos per person per year. But creative chocolatiers like Buosi have a remedy. "What about dipping fresh fruit like bananas, pears or oranges into molten chocolate," he suggests "you can use dark chocolate with cold savoury dishes like smoked sword fish, sea-bass, you can eat cheese with it, add it onto cold rice, smoked duck breast with a chocolate sauce is good too, but there is a limit, pralines dipped into pesto (basil, garlic, olive oil) wouldn't work."

Returning to Acqualagna for a moment, just as it is not really distinguished for anything else but truffles, the Le Marche region as a whole is an underestimated, neglected area of Italy compared to other more famous destinations like Tuscany, Rome, Venice etc. but is packed full of fascinating towns, art, architecture, history, traditions and much more as you can read in the following chapter.

TEN

LE MARCHE

Le Marche (The Marches) is a microcosm of heart-warming, undulating landscapes in central Italy interspersed by picturesque towns and villages packed full of art, history and traditions. Mountains in the west cascade into ripples of hills, rivers traverse parallel valleys before they meet the sea. Ancient townships with wide sandy beaches dotted along the region's 110-mile coastline add further variety. Inexplicably most foreigners shun the area in favour of Italy's more famed destinations. Italians themselves on the other hand flock to the Marches in millions year after year.

Reading about the Marches, I realize some of Italy's best-known personalities were actually born there or after visiting it they never left. I find it irresistible to explore the locations associated with these fascinating personages and head for the coastal city of Pesaro, the birthplace of composer Gioachino Rossini (1792-1868). I have the city's historic core all to myself, it's a hot summer day and virtually everyone is at the beach. From the monumental main square, Piazza del Popolo, a road named after the composer leads to the simple house where he was born. Inside, the same furniture Rossini used and memorabilia relating to his life and work help preserve his memory. I wander around the city, visit the Romanesque cathedral, 15th-century castle and finally find the Rossini theatre where the annual Rossini Opera Festival is in course. Katia Ricciarelli will be singing that evening, the performance is sold out, alas.

Before leaving Pesaro I stroll to the waterfront. So this is where everyone is, in the sea or under beach umbrellas enjoying another sunny day. In a well-tended public garden stands 'La Palla', a bronze sphere, with a crenellated crack in the middle, emerging from a pond. The blue sea acts as the backdrop, the surrounding greenery reflects on the shiny surface. This curious sculpture was created by Arnaldo Pomodoro, one of Italy's most respected contemporary sculptors who's lived, worked and taught in the vicinity of Pesaro most of his life, his just as famed brother Giò Pomodoro unlike his brother was actually born in Pesaro.

  I retreat to my hilltop farmhouse-turned-hotel at the ancient village of San Marcello, overlooking a scenic valley 20 min. drive from the coastal resort town of Senigallia. Despite the distance from the beach, it is full of holiday-makers, excepting a Belgian family they are all Italians in the know who shun fun but overcrowded, noisy resorts along the seaside in favour of these rural, peaceful, guesthouses in or nearby a village where life seems to carry on as it has done for many many centuries. The proprietor Signor Santoni is a friendly, constantly smiling gentleman who wears his hair like Clint Eastwood in his youth, all brushed back. He knows more about the Marches than my two guidebooks put together. He advises me on what is worth seeing and warns. "Forget large cities like the regional capital Ancona, sure they have art and history and interesting monuments but the best is in smaller towns inland. But beware, valleys run vertical to the coast and what seems close on the map necessitates a sort of roller-coaster ride. It's better to drive to the coast and drive back up the next valley."

  "Whatever you do, don't miss Urbino," Santoni insists. This suits me fine, it is the birthplace of the sublime painter Raffaello Sanzio a.k.a. Raphael (1483-1520). Driving through the pretty countryside of vineyards, sunflowers, golden corn, olive groves, freshly ploughed fields and tranquil villages I reach Urbino nestling on a hilltop over 480m (1,600 feet) high. It was founded by duke Federico da Montefeltro in the 15th century as an ideal Renaissance city confined within protective walls. The duke had a palace built and decorated by the leading architects and artists of the day including Raphael's father Giovanni. Urbino is today exactly as it was 500 years ago. The walls, perfectly proportioned

Duke's Palace, churches, palaces, homes, public buildings, the university are so well-restored they seem to have been erected the other day.

The artwork in the sumptuous palace is simply inebriating. I'm particularly struck by Raphael's portrait of a noble woman, The Mute, whose enigmatic expression and identity have kept the experts guessing just like Leonardo's Mona Lisa to this day. Walking up a steep, pink-tinged cobblestone street off-limits to cars I find the unimpressive house where Raphael came to the world marked by a marble plaque and the Italian flag. The artist spent the first 21 years of his life in Urbino, learnt to paint from his father but soon after left for Florence and then went to Rome to serve Pope Julius II for the rest of his short but intensely creative life. Raphael's work is defined as a blend of naturalism and idealism, like Urbino itself.

The food at my guesthouse is abundant and wholesome. "Everything you eat and drink is local" Santoni says. "Even the red wine, Lacrima di Morro D'Alba (the tear of the Moor of Alba) you're drinking comes from those vineyards across the valley. Do you know what that village on the hill behind the vineyards is called?"

" Morro d'Alba?"

"Exactly."

Nobody could explain what the dramatic name of the smooth, flowery tasting wine alludes to.

Following Santoni's indications carefully, I head for Recanati and the holy city of Loreto nearby. Recanati, a quiet town encircled by cultivated sloping fields is doubly rewarding considering two personages of prime importance are associated with it. In the small square, Piazza Sabato del Villaggio, I stand facing the birthplace of poet Giacomo Leopardi (1798-1837), one of the greatest Italian lyrical poets of our times. I join a small group of Italians, who all study the poet's verses at school, converging on the square as if on a pilgrimage and enter the home of Leopardi to visit the formidable library of the poet. After briefly visiting the 16th-century church where he was baptized we finally check out the souvenir/bookstore displaying all of the poets output.

The city's Art Gallery/Museum complex has a surprise in store. There is a section devoted to Beniamino Gigli, another native son of Recanati. Gigli was a tenor as famous as Caruso in his time who performed in 61 operas, appeared in 16 movies between 1935-1951 and sang at New York's Metropolitan for 12 consecutive seasons.

At the holy town of Loreto nearby I join not literary but this time spiritual pilgrims. I'm also on the trail of the gifted Renaissance painter Lorenzo Lotto who, although born in Venice, began his career and spent decades in the Marches finally settling in Loreto where he died at a monastery in 1556, aged 76. The atmospheric main thoroughfare Corso Boccalini leads to the spacious Piazza della Madonna embellished with a monumental fountain. The white marble façade of an imposing, domed church strangely pulls us all towards it. Inside I witness much veneration to Santa Casa (holy house) adorned with statuary depicting early life of Virgin Mary. Inside, the Santa Casa is unadorned with coarse walls, fragments of frescoes and a cross. A black Madonna and Child gaze at us from the altar. We stand there in complete silence, hardly breathing.

I'm surprised to learn that Loreto is a much older site of Roman Catholic pilgrimage than Lourdes in France. According to tradition, in 1291 when Christians faced imminent danger with the fall of the city of Acre in Palestine, the Santa Casa where Jesus, Mary and Joseph lived in Nazareth, was removed by angels to the safety of a hill near Fiume, now in Croatia, and again in 1294 across the Adriatic Sea to the vicinity of Recanati and finally the following year to its present site. Don't ask me how virtually weightless angels managed this hard, physical work. Loreto's holy reputation got a boost when during the second half of 15th-century Pope Paul II granted absolute indulgence to all those who visited the holy house, and began the construction of the church called Il Santuario to house the Santa Casa. In the museum/art gallery of the Santa Casa I find Lorenzo Lotto not only in spirit but also as the author of eight magnificent canvases he painted during the last seven years of his life in Loreto including the masterpieces, Baptism of Christ and Adoration of the Magi. Incidentally, Lourdes became a place of pilgrimage in 1858 when a 14-year-old peasant girl, Bernadette, claimed Madonna appeared to her in a grotto and indicated her where a spring lay. The waters of the spring have been making miraculous cures ever since.

I drive through relaxing agricultural landscapes to Jesi, a sizeable town stretching along a valley, the historic core is still confined within ancient walls just as in numerous other towns in the Marches. The reason being that in the Middle-Ages and beyond, each town was like an independent state called a Marca governed by a duke or a marquis hence the area is called Le Marche in Italian. Jesi's historical protagonist as far as I'm concerned is the composer Giovanni Battista Pergolesi (1710-1736). In the heart of the town I quickly spot Teatro Pergolesi where Jesi's music lovers attend opera. A narrow street named after the composer leads to Jesi's main square lined with fine old buildings, the cathedral and an obelisk. Half way down the street Pergolesi's place of birth is proudly indicated. The brilliant musician that he was, Pergolesi achieved much for such a short life. He is however, most appreciated as a composer of comic operas. His *La Serva Padrona* (1733) became a model for aspiring musicians for generations.

Before I check out, Santoni gives me a quick test to see if I have seen all the 'important' things in the Marches. When I respond negatively to Conero Riviera and the Grotte (caves) di Frasassi he throws his arms in the air. "You can't leave Le Marche without visiting Conero" he says, "it's part of a national park, at the foot of steep emerald hills are white beaches, the sea is so blue you'll think you're in the Caribbean. And what about the Grotte, it took nature thousands of years to sculpt the fantastic stalactites and stalagmites. Most tourists stay on the beaches all the time but take the trouble to go to the Frasassi caves." I comfort Santoni saying I always leave something 'good' behind as an excuse to return. He smiles, heartily shakes my hand and says, "Arrivederci!" I have since then been to Conero and the Grotte, Santoni was absolutely right about everything. There's at least one other place in Le Marche that's worth a mention and that's the township of Fabriano situated in the province of Ancona. The town has been producing quality paper since 14th century not only for printing reading material but also for banknotes, artwork, design and other specialist use. Talking of reading, do you wonder what the state of contemporary Italian literature is, what do Italians like to read these days, how much do they read, which authors are winning awards and making the headlines? It's all revealed in the following chapter.

ELEVEN

READING MATTERS

Let's settle it right from the beginning, Italians don't read that much, the venerable ISTAT keeps churning out figures year after year informing us on how much the average Italian reads. Well, in 2013 those who read at least one book a year stood at 43% of the population, 3% fewer than in 2012; in 2016, it dropped further, to 42.3% reported ISTAT.

A closer, more detailed look reveals that there are wide gender and regional differences, 49.3% of women get through one or more books a year compared to only 36.4% of men who manage to achieve the same result. Those living in the north of the country tend to read more, over 50% do so but when you go south the figure drops to around 30%.

Even so there's a lot of interest in books and up and down Italy numerous, annual book fairs are held to get more people involved. The biggest, and most famous, Salone del Libro, takes place in Turin, in May, which reached its 27th edition in 2014 and was attended by nearly 340,000 book lovers, 10,000 more than the year before. The 30th edition held in 2017 attracted fewer people, only around 141,000, explained by the fact that Milan decided to launch a new, annual book fair itself, Fiera del Libro, in April with many publishers defecting the Turin event but attracted about half the number of people, around 70,000. Book sales at the Turin event in 2014 went up on average by 10-20% compared to 2013, and further still in more recent years, the local media reported. Every year, a bit like Frankfurt book fair, there's a special guest, the literary output of a particular country is chosen, in 2014 Vatican City enjoyed the spot light, in 2015 Germany was the guest of honour. Starting 2016 the organisers rather than a single country, decided to focus on a cultural aspect and hosted, Anime Arabe (Arab souls) and Another Side of America.

Turin event is accompanied by other book fairs that draw huge crowds, including international authors launching Italian version of their book, such as Mantova's Festival Letteratura in early September that's been going strong since 1997. Rome's Festival del Libro e Letteratura kicks off in March, Milan's Bookcity is held in November, Pordenone Festival del Libro goes on show late September, looks like September is a popular month to hold a book fair, in Como, where I live, there's one too, Parolario, a compound deriving from 'parola,' meaning 'word,' and Lario, another name for Lake Como; in the south Italian city of Lecce a book event for kids and young teenagers began in 2013 aiming to generate interest in reading especially among the young and was a success destined to become an annual meeting. The World Book Day, 23 April, is vociferously celebrated. All this effort, hopefully, is going to produce results and increase book readership in Italy, a country so rich in history and culture, but judging by the ISTAT figures for 2016, it just isn't happening.

Italy's publishing world is no longer a series of famous writers publishing a book every year with a famous publisher such as Mondadori, Feltrinelli, Rizzoli, Einaudi, Bompiani and few others, the fluctuating market, also upset by the arrival of e-books, hence easy self-publishing options, means authors old and new have been moving on to new publishers, often small ones, offering better conditions. Let's get one more thing cleared up here, getting published is hard everywhere, for a young, unknown writer to make it big in Italy it is even harder, those who get published are the well-known novelists, or journalists, with strong TV presence either because they are actually hosting a program or they are well-known enough to get invited to TV for an interview or chat show. The only other way is to win one of Italy's literary prizes, a *premio*, most important of which are:

Premio Andersen, set up in 1982 and as the name suggests, is awarded to the best authors and illustrators of children's books. In 2014 the illustrator Alessandro Sanna famed for his picture books won the top award, Fabrizio Silei, a forty something Florentine writer, was deemed the best story teller. There are also prizes for books for different age groups up to 15 years of age and beyond, for instance, in 2017, Pinguino Che Aveva Freddo (penguin who was cold), aimed at up to 6-year-olds, penned by Philip Giordano, won the top prize, in the 6-9-year-old category, La Zuppa dell'Orco (Ogre's soup) by Vincent Cuvellier, was deemed the best.

Premio Bancarella, uncharacteristically this prize was introduced in 1952 by bookshop owners, some of whom had stalls (*bancarella*) at book fairs, and is given to the book not only for its literary but also commercial value, these people are trying to sell books remember. In 2014 Michela Marzano, a philosopher, lecturer, politician born in Rome, 1970, picked up this coveted award for her novel, L'amore è Tutto. È Tutto ciò che So dell' Amore (Love is everything. It's all I know about love). In 2017, Matteo Strukul's book on the Medici dynasty of Florence, I Medici, was the winner.

Premio Bagutta, born in Milan, the heart of the nation's publishing industry, in 1926, this is the oldest book prize in Italy though not as well-known as some of the others and hence with less impact on overall book sales. The 2014 awards went to Milan's, 1945-born port Maurizio Cucchi for his collection of poems, Malaspina. He shared the award with Valerio Magrelli of Rome born in 1957 and lecturer of French literature at Pisa University. Magrelli, essentially a poet, penned his winner, Geologia di un Padre, (geology of a father) not in verse but flowing prose. In 2017, the winning author was, Vivianne Lamarque with her book, Madre d'Inverno (mother of winter).

Premio Campiello, has been awarded since 1962 to the best book of the year and includes a section for young, emerging writers, to help them launch a career in writing. Thirty something Giorgio Fontana born in Saronno, northern Italy, already a winner of prizes for earlier works was awarded this 'premio' for, Morte di un Uomo Felice (death of a happy man), at the 2014 edition, and can truly be defined a new contemporary writer. In 2017, Donatella Di Pietrantonio's book, L'Arminuta, won the top prize.

Premio Italo Calvino, named after the great Italian author (1923 - 1985), was setup in 1985 and is particularly in search of promising, young novelists. The 2013 award went to 1972-born Francesco Maino, a native of a small town, Motta di Livenza, in the Treviso Province of Veneto, for his debut book, Cartongesso (plasterboard), defined by the jury a hybrid mixing novel and essay genres with creative language taking a critical look at his home region, Veneto. The 2016 prizes announced in 2017 went to Elisabetta Pierini for her book, L'Interrutore dei sogni (the dream switch), and Cesare Sinatti for, La Splendente (the splendid).

Premio Mario Luzi, named after the Tuscan poet/author (1914 - 2005), it is unsurprisingly a poetry prize giving out awards in six categories including one coming from a school, a published one, an international one and the most coveted of all an unpublished work which in 2014 went to Daniel Trinca. In 2017 the winner was, Evaristi Seghetta Andreoli for, Inquietudine da Imperfezioni (disquiet caused by imperfections).

Premio Mondello, this Sicilian prize has been awarded to a newcomer since 1975 to support the fledgling novelists especially in Sicily. In 2014 three winners were announced: Irene Chias born in Erice, Sicily, in 1973, but based in Milan, penned, Esercizi di Sevizia e Seduzioni (exercise of violence and seduction) unsurprisingly about a Sicilian family living in Milan; 1967-born Giorgio Falco for a drama, La Gemella H (twin sister H) set in Germany in 1930s involving real estate speculation in Nazi Germany and Italy; and Rome-born Francesco Pecoraro, the veteran writer turning 70 in 2015, for, La Vita in Tempi di Pace (life in time of peace). In 2017, the three winners and their books were: Stefano Massini with Qualcosa sui Lehman (something on Lehman); Alessandra Sarchi with La Notte Ha La Mia Voce (the night has my voice); and Alessandro Zaccuri with Lo Spregio (the disregard).

Premio Strega, probably the best-known of Italy's literary prizes, it was first awarded in 1947 and has a strong impact on sales. It is named not after a literary figure but a grappa brand which sponsors the event. In 2014 Francesco Piccolo, born in 1964 in Caserta, won the top prize with Il Desiderio di Essere come Tutti (the desire to be like everybody else). The 2017 winner was the Milanese author, Paolo Cognetti with, Le Otto Montagne (the eight mountains).

E-book readership is still in its infancy in Italy, even the younger generations although equipped with i-Phones and i-Pads are reluctant to read e-books, or any other kind of books really, however, one reason few e-books are read is also because only around 64% of Italians actually have internet access (ISTAT figures Dec 2014), lowest number in Europe, incredibly late 2014 some 22 million Italians had never gone online. Come 2016 things improved when almost 74% of Italians were reported to have internet access. The other reason for low e-book readership is not many interesting titles were available till a few years ago, now more and more e-books are coming on the market and the choice, and readership, is on the way up, Amazon's Kindle reader can now be bought even in (sizeable) bookshops and shopping centres. Italian book publishers revealed that in 2013 only 63.6% of books published had an e-book version too, come September 2014 the figure jumped to 81.4%, in 2017 nearly all were available also as e-book. Regarding business e-books are creating, in 2011 they only represented 1.2% of total revenues from book sales, come 2016 it went up to around 10%. Despite this new, often cheaper option, for purchasing books, overall sales are not picking up. The slump can also be explained by the economic crisis that began in 2008, that was in fact around the last time a couple of young, new Italian authors, Paolo Giordano (Mondadori 2008) and Silvia Avallone (Rizzoli 2010) were launched in a big way and whose books, La Solitudine dei Numeri Primi (the solitude of primary numbers), and Acciaio (steel) respectively, became best-sellers.

Despite falling readership the number of new titles published in Italy have been going up and up reaching some 66,500 titles in 2016 but few copies, around 2,000, are actually being printed bearing in mind an average book is selling around 1,000 copies a year according to a detailed article published in the Italian weekly news magazine, L'Espresso. Whether published by a famous, big editor like Mondadori or small one, doesn't seem to make much difference to circulation, you can't make people read if they don't want to.

Like elsewhere, Italians are also opting for self-publishing mostly as e-books for its ease and practically zero cost, currently on one of Italy's main e-book publishing platforms, ilmiolibro.it, 20,000 authors are listed, and as elsewhere publishers big and small cannot ignore possible talented writers hiding among them, one publisher, Compton Newton, who began printing low-cost books over a decade ago, is particularly busy scouting for novelists online as do others like Mondadori. Some fairly well-known authors are even going for crowd funding of sorts by publishing a couple or so chapters of their book online for free, and asking readers to contribute €3 if they want to read the rest of the book, if in a month at least €4,000 is raised, the book gets printed if not the readers get their €3 back.

What do Italians like to read? Here's a list of the top 10 bestsellers for 2013.
1. Khaled Hosseini - E l'Eco Rispose (And the Mountains Echoed)
2. Dan Brown - Inferno
3. Roberto Saviani - Zero Zero Zero (non-fiction)
4. Andrea Camilleri - Un Cavo Di Viperi

5. Joel Dicker - La Verità Sul Caso Harry Quebert (La Verité sur l'Affaire Harry Quebert)
6. Fabio Volo - La Strada Verso Casa
7. Massimo Gramellini - Fai Bei Sogni
8. E.L.James - 50 Sfumature Di Grigio (50 Shades of Grey)
9. E.L.James - 50 Sfumature di Rosso (50 Shades of Red)
10. Book based on Walt Disney TV Series, Violetta - Il Mio Diario Un Anno Dopo (My Secret Diary a Year Later)

As you may have noticed there are only four Italian authors among them, all four also appear in TV programs quite frequently: Roberto Saviano is a journalist whose debut book, Gomorrah, on the fictionalised, but extremely realistic, organised crime syndicate, Camorra, based in Naples, became a huge bestseller, Zero Zero Zero is on cocaine trafficking. Andrea Camilleri is a veteran crime fiction writer from Sicily who sets his stories in Sicily; his books starring the police officer, Montalbano, have been made into TV series with enormous success. Fabio Volo is not only a novelist but also an actor/filmmaker and TV personality. Massimo Gramellini is a journalist but is frequently on TV as guest on the popular Fabio Fazio weekend show where he comments on current issues.

Have things changed over the last 4-5 years regarding which authors are being read, see for yourself:

10 bestsellers in 2017 were:
1. Fabio Volo - Quando tutto inizia (when it all starts)
2. Adessoscrivo (a mysterious pseudonym that means, now I write) - Dieci Magnitudo (magnitude 10)
3. Alessandro D'Avenia - Ogni storia è una storia d'amore (every story is a love story)
4. Dan Brown - Origin
5. Francesco Sole - ti voglio bene (I care for you)

6. Alessandro D'Avenia - L'arte di essere fragili (the art of being fragile)
7. Isabel Allende - Oltre l'inverno (beyond winter)
8. Michelle Hunziker - Una vita apparentemente perfetta (an apparently perfect life)
9. Donato Carrisi - L'uomo del labirinto (the man in the labyrinth)
10. Ken Follett - La Colonna di Fuoco (A column of fire)

Commercial aspects apart, Italian writers and particularly poets have made a remarkable contribution to world literature winning no fewer than six Nobel Prizes:
Giosuè Carducci (poet) was the first Italian Nobel laureate, won in 1906
Grazia Deledda (novelist) in 1926
Luigi Pirandello (playwright) in 1934
Salvatore Quasimodo (poet) in 1959
Eugenio Montale (poet) in 1975
Dario Fo (playwright) in 1997

When it comes to worldwide success the top 10 Italian authors are:
1. Dante Alighieri (1265 - 1321) whose Divina Commedia has sold in excess of 20 million copies worldwide, not bad for a poet who's been dead for some 700 years.
2. Carlo Collodi (1826 - 1890) also a Tuscan author like Dante, Collodi is the author of Pinocchio published in 1881 and has sold some 35 million copies and been translated into 200 languages, at least.
3. Carolina Invernizzi (1851 - 1916) was the queen of soap operas which were called feuilleton at the time and derives from the French word for the leaf of a book, feuillet. These non-political, gossipy human stories were printed in newspapers in instalments, Ms Invernizzi managed to pen 123 of these feuilleton becoming also very famous abroad especially in South America

4. Giovannino Guareschi (1908 - 1968), the man behind the still popular Don Camillio series narrating the adventures and misadventures of a priest in rural Italy. The books sold 20 million or so and became a TV series.
5. Andrea Camilleri (b.1925) is the inventor of Commissario Montalbano whose detective stories set in Sicily have been translated into numerous languages and sold over 10 million copies worldwide.
6. Oriana Fallaci (1929 - 2006), another Tuscan writer, a journalist/novelist this time whose non-fiction books are as famous as her novels sold over 20 million copies worldwide. She spent the last five years of her life criticising the extremist Muslim world after the Sep. 11 attack on Twin Towers.
7. Umberto Eco (1932 - 2016), a journalist, historian, intellectual, philosopher who wrote on many subjects but his most famous and international best-seller is Il Nome della Rosa (The Name of the Rose) published in 1980 and sold a staggering 50 million copies around the globe.
8. Giorgio Falletti (1950 - 2014), a musician, stand-up comedian and finally a novelist, Falletti's debut work, a thriller named, Io Uccide (I Kill) published in 2002 was an instant hit and was translated into 30 languages, others followed with similar success.
9. Susanna Tamaro (b.1957), soft spoken, short-haired Tamaro born in Trieste and trained as a filmmaker, made it big with her novel, Và Dove Ti Porta Il Cuore (Follow Your Heart) published in 1994 becoming one of the most successful Italian books ever and selling over 14 million copies worldwide.
10. Roberto Saviano (b.1979), a journalist born in Naples he set his first book, Gomorra, in his native city narrating the hard reality of living with the Camorra. The book was made into a film, then a TV series, and sold over 2.5 million copies in Italy alone. It also disrupted Saviano's life who became the target of Camorra thugs threatening him with death, since the book was published in 2006 he has lived under constant police protection. He contributes

articles to a number of publications: Italian weekly L'Espresso, Time, New York Times, The Times (UK) and Der Spiegel (Germany) among them. Gomorra is now a TV series too.

As everywhere else, Italians don't hesitate to transform a good book into a movie, not necessarily a good one, The Name of the Rose was a big hit everywhere, Follow Your Heart not really but Italy brims with truly talented filmmakers who write their own scripts but what have they been making in recent years? What sort of movies do Italians like?

TWELVE

ITALY'S CINEMA SCENE

Italians may not like reading that much but they do like going to the movies though not necessarily to see Italian films. Save a slight dip in 2008, overall box office takings have been above €600 million per year since 2007 and in 2010 (the Avatar year) it reached an all-time record of about €734 million. For several years before 2007 the figure had always been below the €600 million mark; so despite piracy, the recent economic downturn, and, continuously increasing competition from Smart TV offering on demand movies or subscription streaming options people keep going out to the 'pictures.' One explanation is the growing number of multiplex cinemas offering a wide choice, 3D movies and other services like bars, cafés and restaurants to socialise before and after the screening.

What sort of movies do Italians like anyway? Not that different from what everyone else likes around the globe, big budget Hollywood production taking the lion's share but there are surprises too, small budget Italian comedies especially in recent years have been fighting Hollywood with some success, in 2013 the Italian film, Sole a Catinelle, directed by Gennaro Nunziante, starring Checche Zalone, was the top grossing movie in Italy with takings of €55.3 million, the most successful Italian film ever to be made, and if it weren't for Avatar which grossed €65.7 million, it would be the most successful film ever to be screened in Italy. The second surprise came from another comedy, Il Principe Abusivo, directed by and starring Alessandro Siani which was the 5th most successful film in 2013. Here's the full list of 10 top grossing movies in Italy for the year 2013:

1. Sole A Catinelle - €55.3 million
2. Iron Man 3 - €16 million
3. Frozen - €15.8 million
4. Cattivissimo Me 2 (Despicable Me 2) - €15.3 million
5. Il Principe Abusivo - €14.3 million
6. Fast & Furious - €12.9 million
7. Hobbit - €12.652 million
8. Una Notte Da Leoni 3 (The Hangover 3) - €12.531 million
9. Django Unchanged - €12 million
10. The Croods - €11.5 million

In 2014 five of the above remained in the top 10 despite moving up or down the rankings, Maleficent (4th), The Wolf of Wall Street (8th) and Amazing Spiderman 2 (10th) made the list, Il Principe Abusivo left but was replaced by three Italian movies, all of them comedies: Un Boss in Salotto (5th) directed by Luca Miniero starring the very popular actors Leo Papaleo and Paola Cortellesi; Colpi di Fortuna directed by Neri Parenti famed for his Christmas themed movie series; and Sotto Una Buona Stella (9th) directed and starring Carlo Verdone, and Paola Cortellesi (I did say she was popular).

What about 2016? Checche Zalone was back with another comedy, Quo Vado, again directed by Gennaro Nunziante, again breaking box office records, including his own, with €65.2 million, just short of Avator. The 10 most successful movies in 2016 were:

1. Quo Vado - €65.2 million
2. Star Wars VII - €25.3 million
3. Inside Out - €25.2 million
4. Minions - €23.2
5. Perfetti Sconosciuti - €17.3 million
6. Revenant - €13.8 million
7. Spectre 007 - €12.4 million
8. Captain America - Civil War - €11.2 million
9. Zootropolis - €11 million

10. Il Ponte delle spie (The Bridge of Spies) - €10.8 million

As can easily be seen in the above list English-language movies attract huge crowds but all movies screened at the cinema or TV are dubbed into Italian, Italians don't like reading subtitles. Italian movies, good ones, rarely make it big in the English-speaking world simply because subtitles are used limiting their distribution. Even so when an Italian film wins an Oscar in the Foreign Language section, it does attract much attention also abroad. In 2014 Paolo Sorrentini's La Grande Bellezza won this much coveted award becoming the 14th Italian movie to win an Oscar in this section showcasing the quality of Italy's filmmakers. Here's the list of movies that won an Oscar as best foreign language film:

1. Sciuscià - 1948 by Vittorio de Sica (1901 - 1974)
2. Ladri di Biciclette - 1950 by Vittorio de Sica
3. Le Mura di Malapaga (Au delà des grilles) - 1951 by René Clément (1913 - 1996) an Italy-France co-production
4. La Strada - 1957 by Federico Fellini (1920 - 1993)
5. Le Notti di Cabiria - 1958 by Federico Fellini
6. 8½ - 1964 by Federico Fellini
7. Ieri, Oggi, Domani - 1965 by Vittorio de Sica
8. Indagine Su Un Cittadino al Di Sopra Di Ogni Sospetto - 1971 by Elio Petri
9. I Giardini di Finzi-Contini - 1972 by Vittorio de Sica
10. Amarcord - 1975 by Federico Fellini
11. Nuovo Cinema Paradiso - 1990 by Giuseppe Tornatore
12. Mediterraneo - 1992 by Gabriele Salvatores
13. La Vita È Bella - 1999 by Roberto Benigni
14. La Grande Bellezza - 2014 by Paolo Sorrentini

Another worthy filmmaker, Mario Monicelli (1915 - 2010) whose delightful comedies entertained Italians for decades was nominated six times but never one.

Vittorio de Sica and Federico Fellini took home four Oscars each but each also invented a new language to tell stories. De Sica's simple stories simply but realistically told came to be defined as *neorealismo*, on a small budget he was able to put moving stories on the screen and influenced many generations of filmmakers to come around the world. Fellini moving in quite the opposite direction made long, complex, visually stunning films and as Marcello Mastroianni, who starred in a number of Fellini films put it, "30 years later, people are still wondering what 8½ was about." Breaking away from a linear story line Fellini did challenge orthodox filmmaking traditions making one masterpiece after another. Neapolitan Paolo Sorrentino's La Grande Bellezza is, quite rightly, often likened to a Fellini film but Sorrentino is also very different from Fellini, he has made a movie in English and is planning a new one for 2015, something Fellini never even considered. In 2011 he made, This Must Be the Place, set in Dublin and New York with Sean Penn in the lead role and was busy in 2014 filming, Youth, set in Venice, London and Switzerland starring Michael Caine and Harvey Keitel that hit the screens in 2015. Long before Sorrentini other Italian filmmakers have made films in English; the most noted are probably Sergio Leone (1929 - 2008), master of spaghetti westerns, and Bernardo Bertolucci (b.1941) who impressed the international crowd with works like, The Last Tango in Paris (1972) with Marlon Brando as protagonist, The Sheltering Sky (1990) with John Malkovich and Debra Winger, and The Last Emperor (1987) that went on to win nine Oscars, a 3D version was released in 2012. Bertolucci's latest movie was the adolescent drama, Io e Te (2012), based on a novel by Niccolò Ammaniti and with it the director retuned to making a film in Italian for the first time since his 1981 effort, La Tragedia Di Un Uomo Ridicolo.

Italy has its own 'Oscars' but calls them 'Davide di Donatello' named after a bronze masterpiece by Donatello sculpted in 1440. In the last 10 years, the best Italian movie award went to the following:

2017 - La Pazza Gioa - Paolo Virzì
2016 - Perfetti Sconosciuti - Paolo Genovese
2015 - Anime Nere - Francesco Nunzi
2014 - Capitale Umano - Paolo Virzì
2013 - La Migliore Offerta - Giuseppe Tornatore
2012 - Cesare Deve Morire - Paolo and Vittorio Taviani
2011 - Noi Credevamo - Mario Martone
2010 - L'Uomo Che Verrà - Giorgio Diritti
2009 - Gomorra - Matteo Garrone
2008 - La Ragazza Del Lago - Andrea Molaioli

In recent years more Italian filmmakers are opting for English language films with international settings and international stars, after all the movie will be dubbed into Italian and released in Italy too. Gabriele Muccino is one such filmmaker. Born in Rome in 1967, Muccino's first success was the romantic comedy, L'Ultimo Bacio, in 2001, five years later ambitious Muccino was in Hollywood making a big-budget movie, The Pursuit of Happiness, followed by, Seven Pounds, in 2008 both starring Will Smith both big hits at the box office. After yet another Hollywood hit, Playing for Keeps (2012), Muccino was busy filming, Fathers and Daughters, in 2014, starring Russell Crowe, which was released in 2015. Oscar winner Giuseppe Tornatore also stands out; born in Sicily in 1956, he made, The Legend of 1900 (1998) in English with Tim Roth and Pruitt Taylor Swift playing the lead roles, in nearly three hours of viewing, we're told the story of a pianist who spends his entire life on an ocean liner. In 2006 Tornatore returned with, The Unknown Woman, and in 2013 he made the romantic mystery, The Best Offer, set in Italy, Vienna and Prague starring Geoffrey Rush, Jim Sturgess, Sylvia Hoeks and Donald Sutherland. His next project was yet another English-language film, The Correspondence, filmed in 2015 using A-list British and American actors. Shooting movies in English with internationally well-known actors obviously makes sense, it appeals to more people, draws larger numbers of cinema-goers across the world. Other Italian filmmakers are opting for this like Luca Guadagnino who made, A Bigger Splash, an erotic thriller with Tilda Swinton, Ralph Fiennes and Dakota Johnson in the lead set on the small island of Pantelleria, off the coast of Sicily, which debuted in 2015 at Venice Film Festival. Gudagnino was back in 2017 with, Call Me With Your Name, a much acclaimed effort set in the Northern Italian city of Crema, where the director is based, starring Armie Hammer and Timothée Chalamet. Also in 2017, another gifted Italian filmmaker, Paolo Virzì made an English-language movie, Ella and John - The Leisure Seeker, starring Helen Mirren and Donald Sutherland. Then there's Saverio Costanzo who brought Hungry Hearts to Venice Film Festival 2014 with the Italian actress Alba Rohrwacher playing alongside emerging US star Adam Driver (appeared in the Star Wars VII in 2016). Costanzo took an Italian story, Il Bambino Indaco, set in Padoa, penned by Marco Franzoso, and took it to New York. Matteo Garrone after making the highly successful Gomorra (2008) based on Roberto Saviano's namesake bestseller followed by Reality (2012) in Italian decided to make his new film, 'The Story of Stories' based on 17th-century fairy tales written by Giambattista Basile, in English using international stars Salma Hayek, Vincent Cassell and Toby Jones as protagonists.

     This of course doesn't mean there's no interest in Italian-language movies abroad even if subtitled, or dubbed into the local language in many countries. The gifted Tuscan, filmmaker Paolo Virzì's 11th film, Il Capitale Umano, made in 2014, has been sold to 30 countries. Andrea Camilleri's Comissario Montabano TV Series that reached its 9th season in 2013 has been screened in 17 countries from Argentina to France to Russia, UK and USA. During 2014 in at least four Italian language films were being planned or made with the participation of international stars such as Juliette Binoche appearing in Piero Messina's debut work, L'Attesa,' Sharon Stone was acting for Pupi Avati in, Un Ragazzo d'Oro, John Turturro was participating in two films, the great Roman filmmaker and winner of many awards, Nanni Moretti's, Mia Madre, and Marco Pontecorvo's, Tempo Instabile Con Probabili Schiarite. Is this a fad? Not really, Luchino Visconti's masterpiece, Gattopardo (1963) had Alain Delon and Burt Lancaster alongside Claudia Cardinale; Bertolucci's epic, Novenecento (1976) had the likes of Robert De Niro, Gérard Dépardieu and again Burt Lancaster.

When it comes to all-time movie hits, out of the 10 top grossing films ever to be screened in Italy five are Italian movies:

1. Avatar (2010) - €65.7 million
2. Quo Vado - €65.2 million
3. Sole A Catinelle (2013) - €55.3 million
4. Titanic (1997) - €50.2 million
5. Che Bella Giornata (2011) - €43.5 million
6. La Vita È Bella (1998) - €31.2 million
7. Alice in Wonderland (2010) - €30.4 million
8. Benvenuti Al Sud (2010) - €29.9 million
9. L'Era Glaciale (Ice Age) (2009) - €29.7 million
10. Il Codice Da Vinci (2006) - €28.7 million

Despite taking the 5th place in Italy, Roberto Benigni's La Vita È Bella, a brilliant comedy set in a concentration camp, with takings of $57 million at the box office remains the top grossing Italian movie abroad. The other four all have stand-up comedians/actors playing the lead. Sole A Catinelle and Che Bella Giornata were directed by Gennaro Nunziante with Checco Zalone, also a musician, playing the lead, both the actor and director were born in the south Italian city of Bari and also made Cado Dalle Nubi in 2009 which was another major hit. Benvenuti al Sud was made by

Neapolitan filmmaker Luca Miniero with the popular comedians Claudio Bisio and Alessandro Siani playing the lead. Neapolitan Siani went on to make his first film as director, Il Principe Abusivo with amazing results, placed fifth most successful film in 2013, his new effort, Si Accetano Miracoli, was screened in Jan 2015. Chiedimi Se Sono Felice had the comedian trio Aldo, Giovanni, Giacomo, three brilliant stand-up comedians who pack the theatres across Italy every time they go on tour; they've also made several films together which were released around Christmas time with excellent box office success every time.

When the movie is finished, the 'wrap' is celebrated but what sort of bubbly is chosen? The local spumante, its cousin prosecco, or the more sophisticated sounding, and famous, French champagne? Italians are proud of their bubbly brands and are likely to pop the cork of one of theirs to celebrate; judging by sales figures abroad, spumante in recent years seems to be overtaking champagne in a number of countries, but what's the difference between the two anyway? And interestingly is there an organic version of spumante? What is organic wine anyway?

THIRTEEN

SPUMANTE AND ORGANIC WINE

In 2014, according to International Organisation for Vine and Wine, Italy lost first place to France as the world's top wine producer. With an output estimated at 46.1 mhl (million hectolitres) France took the lead, Italy with 44.6 mhl came second. But not regarding spumante, the bubbly white wine, which a number of countries across the world preferred to champagne and hence imported and consumed more. Figures released early 2014 showed that against 440 million bottles of spumante Italy produced France managed 349 million bottles of champagne. Export values are also different whereas Italy exported 80% of its produce France exported 45%; meanwhile China imported twice as much spumante in 2013, UK 50%, Russia 31% and USA 24% more than in 2012. At home 86% of Italians celebrate special occasions, Christmas and New Year in particular, with a spumante and only 11% opt for champagne. Come 2016 Italian wine production increased to 50.1 mhl overtaking France again where production stood at 47.9 mhl; wine exports, spumante in particular, continued rising, ironically, according to Coldiretti, Italy's main agricultural organization, France imported three times as much spumante compared to 2015, whereas champagne imports to Italy remained more or less the same, in other words, for every bottle champagne popped in Italy, six spumante was opened in France. How things will stand in 2017 is too soon to tell but a bad year for all has been forecast with worldwide wine production dropping by over 8%.

How exactly is spumante (literally bubbly) made and what differentiates it from champagne? Italy's bubbly comes in two main categories, the sweet type made with grapes like Moscato, Malvasia and Brachetto, and the dry one usually made with

Chardonnay or Pinot Noir grapes. What's known as prosecco is a dry fizzy wine like spumante but is produced in the Friuli Venezia Giuglia region in the north east of Italy. Champagne is a dry wine made with Chardonnay, Pinot Noir and Pinot Meunier grapes. Production method is also different, Most of Italian Spumante is produced employing the so- called Charmat method whereby the wine is fermented for a second time in tanks and then bottled. Despite its name this method was invented by Federico Martinotti (1860 - 1924) in Asti, Piemonte, but was patented by the Frenchman Eugène Charmat in 1910, sometimes it is called Charmat-Martinotti method. Champagne is produced by the so-called Chamepenois method whereby after primary fermentation the wine is bottled, yeast added and a second fermentation takes place in the bottle. This is a more labour intensive method as the bottles are periodically twisted by hand to ensure good fermentation. Cheap spumante is also made by the addition of carbon dioxide and is indicated on the bottle. Champenois method tends to produce smaller bubbles, considered more refined, better tasting, compared to added carbon dioxide or the Charmat method. Needless to say due to hand picking of grapes, production method which requires longer ageing, and let's include the 'fame' factor, champagne is more expensive but there are also up market spumante too like Prosecco, Ferrari or Berlucchi (rosé). What is pushing spumante exports is probably its lower price compared to champagne otherwise only the wealthy would celebrate special occasions with the all important bubbly.

Over the last decade or so organic wine production has been gaining ground especially in Italy. As demand for organically grown food increased, wine producers began investing in organic wine too. Is it possible to have organic spumante? In a word, yes. According to Slow Food wine guide, 2015, of the 2,000 or so winemakers considered, 590 were making organic wine including spumante and prosecco. Italy's federation of organic food and wine makers has reported that 53,000 hectares of vineyards are used for making organic wine, Sicily leads the way followed by Tuscany, Puglia, Abruzzo, Emilia Romagna and Le Marche but there's also production in other regions. Over the last 6 -7 years there's been a substantial increase, the 2014 edition of the Slow Food guide listed 450 organic wineries, the 2009 edition of, *La Guida ai Vini Bio*, the most comprehensive, authoritative organic wine guide in Italy, listed 713 wines produced by only 184 different winemakers across the nation and 'only' 34,000 hectares of land was devoted to organic viticulture in Italy, more than any other European country, save Spain which leads the way with 57,000 hectares. Coldiretti reported that in 2009 there were some 4,000 wineries making organic wine in Italy. Regions like Sicily and Puglia are particularly active also because the dry hot climate of southern Italy favours organic farming as no fungicides are necessary for instance.

What exactly is organic wine anyway? By definition it is wine made with organically grown grapes and as in all organic farming no synthetic chemicals are used, a wide range of pesticides, fertilisers and fungicides which may be tolerated in ordinary viticulture are banned. Close up, it is a delicate art as Valentino Paladin, founder of Bosco del Merlo winery, one of the largest in Veneto region which makes organic versions of Prosecco, Pinot Grigio, Cabernet etc., explained, "Organic wine starts life well before the *vendemmia* (grape harvest), it starts with the vineyard design, with the type of vines that must suit the particular soil and climate, and the density of the vines. A robust plant will be better equipped to resist adverse conditions. The first intervention is in late autumn when pruning takes place to reduce the number of buds so as to favour a more vigorous growth. In February natural fertilisers derived from beetroot molasses are added. In May the vine leaves are checked and treated with algae based products to keep away harmful insects, if this fails, sulphur, lime or copper based chemicals are used to defend the vines. Undergrowth is cleared every 15 days and left on the ground to attract useful insects like ladybirds. Come June the so-called green *vendemmia* is done to reduce the number of grape bunches which will limit competition and allow the concentration of 'noble' ingredients in the remaining grapes. At the end of July the leaves on the vine shoots are removed and the shoots are tied above the grapes to allow the sun to reach them, in August if the weather's too dry, the soil is tilled to release moisture into the soil. Next comes the *vendemmia*."

How seriously is organic wine taken? *La Guida ai Vini Bio* and Slow Food employ professional wine tasters to try the wines coming from all the wineries, all certified as organic, and evaluate their merits. In their 2009 evaluation *La Guida ai Vini Bio*'s wine tasters, after trying all 713, named 114 wines as worthy of special mention headed by 34 wines from Tuscany, 17 from Veneto and 12 from Piemonte. A 2006 white from Soave, an extensive wine-making area in Veneto, was deemed the best. Arturo Socchetti, the president of the consortium of winemakers in Soave, commented, "The success of the Soave shows that quality in our region has grown in all directions, producing organic wine is complex and challenging, which, without letting it go to our heads, I'm pleased to say we have won thanks to wines that not only taste good but also satisfy clients who are more and more concerned with health and appreciate organic wine for it."

For the last 25 years the biggest organic food fair in Europe known as BioFach has been held every Feb. in Nurnberg, Germany; in the 2009 edition 318 organic wine makers from 23 nations took part, 94 of them, the largest representation, were from Italy. Altogether the exhibitors showcased 521 wines, again with 152 wines Italy outnumbered everyone. Some 40 wine experts, sommeliers and journalists awarded prizes to the best. Italy took home some of the top prizes, a gold special for Soave Doc "Pieve vecchia", a gold medal for Recioto di Soave Docg "San Zeno," a silver medal for Soave Doc "Borgoletto" and three other silvers for wines from Emilia Romagna. By 2013 the total number of gold and silver medals obtained by Italy reached 36, meanwhile competition from other winemaking countries increased pushing Italy to the 4th place in the overall medal winners' rankings, France took the lead with 61, Germany 51 and Spain with 42 wins. At the 25th edition of the event in 2014 2,235 organic food and wine producers from 76 countries took part, Italy with 348 participants was by far the largest group after Germany.

Organic wine making is hard work, harvest is done entirely by hand, the yields are lower than for ordinary vineyards and consequently organic wines tend to cost 10 to 20% more. The final result does not necessarily taste better either. Why bother make it in the first place? Andrea Cecchi, who runs the Tuscan winery, Cecchi with brother Cesare, explains, "We make organic versions of our Chiantis too, such as the Natio, it is a niche market for people who espouse the philosophy behind organic food and drink, they, quite rightly, consider organic produce healthier for themselves and the environment. It also helps vegetarians and vegans who when selecting a wine look for those that are made without the use of any animal by-products like albumen, gelatine and casein which are sometimes used to fine a wine to remove organic particles that may make the wine cloudy. Because we wanted Natio to be vegan friendly, we chose to use Bentonite, a natural clay product, to fine it. This inert substance is added to the vat and as it sinks to the bottom, the clouding particles cling to it, making the wine clear and attractive."

Getting from organically grown grapes to wine in the bottle involves other challenges for the wine maker. To keep the grapes fresh and free of bacterial attack, sulphur dioxide (SO_2) gas is normally used. But this being a synthetic chemical should be avoided in organic wines, SO_2 is also added in liquid form to wines especially whites to act as a preservative, reds contain tannins which have anti-bacterial properties and necessitate less SO_2. Alas, SO_2 can cause headaches and allergies. As a better substitute has not yet been found, a compromise has been reached, according to EU rules until 2012 20 mg per litre less SO2 was being used in organic wines compared to normal wine, as of 2012 SO2 had to be at least 30-50 mg per litre lower than in conventional equivalents. Meanwhile, Chemical and Industry journal has recently published a study by the Cartagena University whereby scientists have found that replacing SO2 by Ozone produces the same anti bacterial results in 90% of the cases. They also found that Ozone-treated grapes had four times more anti-oxidant properties but they couldn't explain why.

There are other details to think about. Grape harvest is done in small quantities, bunches are not piled up or allowed to press on each other to prevent damage and untimely fermentation. Pressing of the grapes is done softly to avoid any pollutants on the grape skins to enter the vinification process which is started without delay by adding wild yeast. The room temperature is carefully monitored to avoid any interference with the fermentation process and perhaps the proliferation of undesired bacteria. No additives should be used to eliminate cloudiness, by patiently waiting the particles
suspended in the liquid will deposit to the bottom. In normal wine making this process is accelerated by adding fining chemicals to coagulate the unwanted particles and clarify the wine.

Judging by the huge number in *Guida ai Vini Bio*, Slow Food and the number of such wineries taking part in BioFach, organic wine making has taken a huge step forward, just like other organic farming products. Perhaps because "Nature is right," as Hagen Sunder, co-founder of BioFach with Jürgen Ries, said at a recent opening ceremony. "In the same way that the flapping of a bird's wings can trigger off a hurricane, may BioFach trigger off a hurricane of sustainability for the benefit of all," was Jürgen Ries comment at the same venue.

Organic agriculture is of course good news for the environment, less or no chemical pesticides or fertilisers can only benefit the ecological standing of a nation and reduce health hazards for the people. Banning the use of chemicals is of course only one of the ways to safeguard the environment, what else is Italy doing? How green is it, bearing in mind the EU nations, including Italy, agreed in Oct 2014 to cut greenhouse emissions by 40% by 2030 compared to 1990.

FOURTEEN

HOW GREEN IS ITALY?

If you were to visit north of the country, especially the so-called *Pianura Padana*, a vast plain extending across Lombardy, parts of Piemonte, Veneto and down to Emilia-Romagna regions, Italy would seem densely populated, overbuilt, highly industrialised, which it is all that in these parts, but overall Italy is far from turning into an asphalt jungle. Despite the building frenzy that began in 1950s, a third of Italy is still covered with trees, actually over the last 50 years the size of woods and forests has increased by nearly 18% as reported by Enrico Pompei, the head of national forestry inventory, Inventario Forestale Nazionale (IFN), on the science pages of the Italian weekly, L'Espresso, Aug. 2014.

Monitoring of Italy's wooded, agricultural areas began in 1954 by L'Istituto Geografico Militare based in Florence. Comparing the data obtained then with those of 1995 and 2005 as well as even more recent information supplied by AGEA (Agenzia delle Erogazione in Agricoltura), a state organisation that assesses Italy's agricultural capacity and production levels, Pompei observed that wooded areas have actually increased due to abandonment of fields once used for agriculture such as vineyards, fruit orchards and olive groves as well as pastures. This doesn't really come as a surprise, just after WWII almost half the nation's workforce was employed in farming, in the 21st century about 3% of Italians still work in agriculture, actually judging by the latest figures supplied by Caritas, the charity organisation that supplies Italy's immigration data, out of around one million farm workers in 2013, 322,000 or so were foreigners. As a result woods have been encroaching all this abandoned land, for instance down the southern coast of Tuscany oak and black locust woods have grown, in Sardinia's inland eucalyptus and cork oak have gained much ground, in mountainous areas of Italy harbouring conifers, especially pines, and spruce have expanded. All this is good news of course, Italy met the Kyoto Protocol requirements easily. In force starting 2005, this international agreement on climate change asked the countries taking part to commit to cutting back harmful emissions between 2008 and 2012, Italy did its share by cutting back 7%, half a point more than required. In 2013 greenhouse gas emissions went down by further 7.8% reported by Italy's Sustainable Development Foundation. All this was effortlessly achieved thanks to woods and forests absorbing 11% of the emissions in question saving the nation some €200 million a year, the sum Italy would have had to pay as fine and spend on technology etc. to bring about the needed reduction. Over the last two decades, woods reclaimed 6% of the land, in Central Italy, in the hilly, mountainous regions of Abruzzo, Umbria and Le Marche, not only unused farmland but also abandoned villages have been overtaken by woods. The same happened in Sicily and to prevent more villages dying out, some municipalities have recently begun giving property away to all those who undertake to restore old houses to bring back some life back to these fast emptying rural areas. In the future this expansion is expected to continue but at a slower rate of about 0.3% a year. The reduced rate of expansion is soon explained by the fact that there won't be much space left beyond the outskirts of towns, cities and the edges of roads to reclaim.

What may be good for removing green house gases can also cause harm in unexpected ways. Woods growing out of control with little maintenance has led to serious floods especially in Liguria where over the last 80 years some 70% of the region has been taken over by trees, ageing, heavy branches fell on the ground, blocking streams and general drainage when rain fell. The years 2011, 2014 and 2016 were particularly bad for Liguria when streams and rivers broke their banks and flooded some areas of the regional capital Genoa causing fatalities and a lot of material damage. But things are, slowly, changing, maintenance of woods by removing broken branches, fallen trees, undergrowth is improving, drainage to safeguard from floods but also preventing fires and creating economic opportunities in a number of regions. In Le Marche and Parma area for instance, favourable conditions are being created for truffle cultivation and mushroom growth. The wood and dried plant material are being fed into biomass heating plants to make renewable, sustainable energy. According to International Energy Agency in 2002 Italy was producing 1200 Megawatts of energy from biomass, not that much compared to UK, Germany and Spain for example who were producing three times as much at the time, but Italy is catching up fast, in 2009 just over 2000 Megawatts were being produces, in 2012 some 800 plants across the nation were pumping over 3000 biomass Megawatts. Judging by the expansion of its woods and forests, Italy can potentially increase this renewable energy production exponentially, in 2014 there were already 1,200 plants mostly in rural areas making Italy the third largest producer of biogas in the world. Over the preceding five years some €4.5 billion had been invested in biogas production creating 12,000 jobs. Besides biomass Italy has made a huge effort to increase 'clean' energy output, solar panels have been installed on roofs and in unused fields, wind farms have sprung up, government has been offering massive tax incentives for everyone to convert to more efficient eco-friendly insulation and heating systems, to cars that run on methane gas rather than petrol, obtaining good results, as of 2013, 10% of energy produced came from renewable sources placing Italy fifth behind Ireland, Switzerland, UK and Denmark among the 34-member OECD countries. What's Italy criticised about is that it is more a consumer of 'green technology' rather than a producer of one. As the second strongest manufacturer in Europe after Germany not much investment has gone into green technology explained by the fact that some 90% of Italian companies count fewer than 15 employees each and lack the type of spending power needed.

The growth of wooded areas is not proceeding evenly, as mentioned earlier, highly industrialised areas in Lombardy and Veneto have seen a modest increase in their woods, around 2.8% and 5.8% respectively, and that was only in the mountainous areas. Down on the plains and large urban areas no such growth has been observed, on the contrary, intensive farming and on-going building frenzy is contracting woodlands. Some effort has gone into planting new trees and helping the local populace to maintain woods. Over the last decade or so three small forests have grown in Lombardy, namely Bigarello, in the province of Mantua, Settimo Milanese and Pioltello near Milan. Hopefully more will be done in these massively built up areas to reduce pollution, greenhouse gases and improve quality of life at the same time.

To do just that all major cities, headed by Milan, now have car and bicycle-share schemes, more and more cities big and small are building bicycle lanes. As of 2014 there are some 80,000 km of bicycle lanes up and down the country, including rural areas, around lakes, along rivers, for commuting to work, school etc as well as recreation. Ironically the most built-up area, Lombardy, has nearly 1,200 km of such lanes, more than any other region, second placed Tuscany boasts just under 700 km and with around 640 km Veneto comes in third. Compared to northern European nations, the figures are not that impressive but ecology, pollution reduction, global warming are familiar concepts in Italy too and both the government, especially at municipality level, and the people are well aware of the issues involved. All Italian town centres are free of motorised traffic these days, and the pedestrian only areas in towns and cities have done nothing but grow over the last decade or two. Meanwhile, other revolutionary, ecological buildings are literally on the rise; to coincide with the Universal Expo that kicked off in May 2015 in Milan, a 6-storey pavilion called, Palazzo Italia, was inaugurated at the Expo site, the special cement used on the outside of the building was of the breathing type and cleaned the air as well.

    What about recycling? How does Italy fare with the rest of Europe? According to Eurostat figures, in 2012 EU nations on average recycled 42% of their waste, Italy was just below the average with 38%. The EU requires all its members to recycle 50% of their waste by 2020. Italy not only met the target, in 2017, according to Eurostat again, it became the most successful in EU with nearly 77% of its waste recycled, France was placed second with 54% and UK 3rd with 44%. Regions mostly in North Italy plus Le Marche and Sardinia had already reached this target, three other regions, Val d'Aosta, Umbria and Emilia Romagna, were nearly there. In 2011 Italy was among the first countries to ban plastic carrier bags replacing them with biodegradable alternatives, over the next three years even the use of these biodegradable bags was halved, people simply switched to carriers that can be used over and over. Just as averages in the Eurostat only give an approximate figure and do not reflect reality for each country, in some parts of Germany for instance recycling is at 65% but as a national average it was 43% in 2017. In Italy too there are regional variations, in some municipalities in the north of the country recycling level was not far from that of Germany. In Como where I'm based we've been separating glass, paper, aluminium and plastic for over a decade, come summer 2014 we began separating also organic waste to be transformed into compost, and over the following year or two we were on target to recycle 65% of our rubbish. Quantity of waste produced in Italy between 2011 and 2014 went down from 31.4 million tons to 29.6 million tons and over the same period 4.6% more recyclable waste was collected. Whether this was due to diligence or a consequence of reduced expenditure by consumers struggling with the economic downturn is hard to say. Collecting rubbish and separating it is one thing, recycling is another and there are wide, regional variations in how much of the waste ends up in rubbish tips anyway. The research group Althesys which supplies figures to Italian government on waste management issues, reported that in 2014 average recycling level in Italy had improved to 42.3% but in Calabria, Lazio, Liguria, Puglia and Sicily some 90% of waste collected for recycling was still being dumped into gigantic tips that are dangerously close to full capacity. Incinerators are of course being built to handle urban waste, unfortunately only 20% of the total planned have actually been built and to meet international commitments regarding waste management, Italy will have to spend €15 billion by 2030.

Recycling isn't only good for the environment, reduces global warming, improves the quality of air we breathe, it also saves money and creates jobs. The general manager of Althesys, Alessandro Marangoni, speaking to Italian daily, La Repubblica, explained, "A study carried out in 9 EU countries on the benefits of recycling only the PET bottles found that over five years €5.5 billion was saved, €1.2 billion of which in Italy," and estimated that when all 28 EU nations reached the 50% recycling target, it will create 875,000 jobs . "By only recycling packaging materials, €2.2 billion a year can be saved on energy expenditure," Marangoni reassured.

Waste can also turn into artwork, in Nov. 2013 an exhibition of 40 such artworks was held in Rimini as a sideline to Ecomondo, an ecologists' fair on sustainability, recycling etc. From all over Italy, and elsewhere, 'trash art' was proudly displayed as a variation of modern art. Yes, despite its fame for all sorts of art from Roman period frescoes to Renaissance paintings filling museums and adorning historical monuments, Italy is also becoming famous for new modern art museums and temporary exhibitions.

FIFTEEN

ITALY'S TOURIST TRADE

According to data supplied by United Nations World Tourism Organisation (UNWTO), and analysed by Bank of Italy, 47.7 million tourists descended on Italy in 2013, some 4 million more than in 2012, making Italy the 5th most popular tourist destination in the world bringing $41.1 billion worth of revenues to the country, 3.1% more than in 2012. Come 2016 the number of visitors jumped to 50.7 million consolidating Italy's position as the fifth most visited country in the world. It is welcome upturn supplying much needed jobs too, currently some 2.7 million people in Italy work in tourism which generates 4.2% of GDP. In case you're wondering, about 40% of these tourists came from just three countries: Germany, USA and France followed by UK in 4th place.

What do all these millions of people look for? No prizes for guessing that they seek Italian culture and history, awesome monuments, archaeological sites, immense artistic heritage, fashion, the beaches along the Adriatic coast, in Puglia and Sicily, and most probably Italian food and wine. Apart from beach life and sightseeing many tourists end up in a museum or art gallery and again the choice is vast. Over the previous years the rankings have changed little if at all. Around 44.5 million admission tickets were sold in 2016 to enter Italy's top 30 state-owned museums, up from 36 million in 2013, bringing in some €172 million in fees. However, Vatican Museum in Rome, obviously not owned by the Italian state, alone attracted 5.5 million visitors earning a staggering €88 million from ticket sales alone in 2013; in 2016 the number visitors rose still to 6.07 million. Here are the top 10 most visited sites in 2016 and how many visitors they attracted

1. Colosseum - Rome - 6.41 million
2. Pompei - Naples - 3.28 million
3. Uffizi - Florence - 2.01 million
4. Galleria Dell'Accademia - Florence - 1.46 million
5. Castel Sant'Angelo - Rome - 1.23 million
6. Venaria Reale Palace - Turin - 1.01 million
7. Capodimeno - Naples - 1.00 million
8. Florence Museums - (in addition to the two above) - 881,460
9. Egyptian Museum - Turin - 852,540,000
10. Miramare Castle - Trieste - 833, 300

How do these numbers compare with other famous museums abroad, again according to UNWTO, in 2013 Louvre in Paris attracted 9.2 million visitors, British Museum the same as Colosseum, 5.63 million or so, come 2016 visitors to Louvre decreased to 7.4 million but to Colosseum increased to 6.41 million and British Museum to 6.42 million.

Italy's ambitious culture minister, Dario Franceschini, has introduced some interesting changes that led to 7% increase in the number of visitors during the three months Jul.-Aug. 2014 alone, that's 400,000 more paying admissions. How did he do this? He abolished free admission to the over-65 residents in EU, extended opening hours, on Fridays you can visit major museums till 10 pm, and to attract, and promote, museums and art galleries first Sunday of each month he abolished admission charge which resulted in 50% increase in visitors to the Colosseum, to a lesser extent the same happened to other top tourist attractions. Franceschini wants to go well beyond that, he lamented that some 80% of Italy's museums don't even have a gift shop, let alone a café. With all the art, history and beauty southern Italy holds, only 15% of tourists venture south of Rome, Franceschini wants to change that too; as if to lend him a hand, the southern Italian town of Matera where Mel Gibson set his 2004 box office hit, The Passion of The Christ, was voted the European City of Culture 2019 which will bring investment, infrastructure and hopefully tourists to the area. Italy, Franceschini pointed out, spends only 0.11% of its GDP to promote tourism, less than half of what France does, that should be changed, and as Prime Minister Matteo Renzi pointed out it should be massively increased to 1% of GDP. Funds to run museums etc are distributed equally to all local authorities regardless of performance, in future the culture minister wants to give money to museums based on performance, more ticket sales more funds, which should give an incentive to superintendents to promote tourism in their area and attract more visitors. In Jan 2015 Italian government actually placed job ads in The Economist seeking 20 managers for the nation's top 20 museums arguing a museum should employ a manager, a CEO, like in any other field to run the tourist attraction as any business and create revenue, and jobs along with it. This was successfully introduced in Turin where the Egyptian Museum is run as a collaboration between the state and private firms. As a matter of fact, firms already supply services to state-owned museums and art galleries up and down the country in the form of audio-guides, guided visits, cafés, bookshops, booking services etc but the commission earned by the state for these services hasn't produced much income for the state, in 2013 over 85% of takings went to the firms. Funds from private citizens and/or firms are also welcome to restore crumbling monuments in exchange for publicity, one good example of this private/public collaboration is taking place in Rome where the fashion shoemaker, Diego Della Valle, the man behind the Hogan and Tod's brands, has given €25 million to restore the Eternal City's most famous monument, the Colosseum. A Japanese businessman recently paid for the restoration of Rome's Pyramid of Cestius erected in 12 BC, in exchange the humble Japanese asked for a small plaque bearing his name to be placed by the monument. There are tax incentives being fine tuned to allow donations for art, monument and museum restoration; 65% of the money spent will be tax deductible. Investment, involvement in the country's tourist industry is also extended to the younger generations by giving them tax incentives to start up anything from agritourism concerns to bed and breakfast businesses.

A closer look at what Italy offers in terms of tourist attractions reveals some bewildering information, as of 2017 the number of UNESCO World Heritage Sites in Italy has risen to 53, more than any other country in the world. ISTAT informs that there are 4,588 museums in Italy, of which 240 are archaeological sites and 501 monuments or ensembles of monuments such as the Forum in Rome. One would think all that would be enough to keep any tourist busy for a lifetime but there are other attractions still for art lovers: temporary exhibitions. What's new about that? It's the sheer size of the offer again that dazzles, in 2012 some in 3,650 art exhibitions were inaugurated virtually all across Italy, that's 10 a day. Again what's surprising is the type of art on display, in 58% of the cases it was modern, or contemporary art, i.e. 19th, 20th and 21st century works.

Let's take a closer look at which exhibitions, or artists, drew the most crowds. The most successful exhibition in 2014 was on the Dutch artist, Johann Vermeer (1632 - 1675) whose masterpiece, Girl with a Pearl Earring, displayed in Bologna, attracted 362,000 art lovers. Impressionists are nearly always a hit in Italy, like everywhere else. Back in 2006 in Turin, when the Winter Olympic games came to the city, 'Impressionists and Snow' theme sold 300,000 tickets; 'From Botticelli to Matisse' exhibition in Verona, and 'Towards Monet' in Vicenza held in 2012 and 2013 respectively, attracted some 700,000. Italian great, Titian (1485 - 1570), whose 50 paintings were shown in Scuderie del Quirinale in Rome, in 2013, didn't quite much the success of the Impressionists but was seen by 270,000, more success came in 2014 with the works of Mexican painter, Frida Kahlo (1907 -1954) but so far the biggest success at Scuderie was achieved in 2010 with Caravaggio (1571 - 1610) when 600,000 came to see his striking paintings. It is argued that it's easy to have success in a city like Rome visited by some 30 million tourists a year but the following year when Lorenzo Lotto's work was exhibited in the Scuderie it attracted a third of what Caravaggio managed. Meanwhile in 2014 Ferrara put on a retrospective on Henri Matisse selling 125,000 tickets not bad for a small city. As autumn 2014 came Scuderie celebrated the 15-century, Flemish artist Hans Fleming with an exhibition of his paintings from 11 Oct. to 18 Jan 2015; also over autumn 2014 in Milan's Palazzo Reale Van Gogh, Chagall and Segantini were on display and in Vicenza between 24 Dec. 2014 and 2 Jun. 2015 a night themed exhibition going from Tutankhamen to Van Gogh was in course, Frida Kahlo meanwhile moved from Rome to Genoa between 20 Sep. 2014 and 8 Feb. 2015 making sure there was no shortage of art exhibitions across the nation. In 2016 the five most visited exhibitions were: Floating Piers by Christo on Lake Iseo attracted 2.5 million people over two weeks. The second was Biennale Architecture held in Venice attracting 260,000, followed by the exhibition on the Belgian contemporary visual artist, Jan Fabre, in Florence with 254,000 visitors, fourth came, From Impressionists to Picasso, held in Genoa attracting 250,000 and the fifth was naïf artist Antonio Ligabue (1899 - 1965) showcased in Palermo with 210,000 flocking to see his works.

  The increasing demand for modern/contemporary art means more and more such permanent museums and art galleries are being opened in Italy, one of the latest was inaugurated in Florence in June 2014 dedicated to 20th century art, bringing the total of such venues in Italy to around 40. Incidentally there are three other modern art museums in Florence. Nationwide, the number is certainly more than 40, for instance Capodimonte Museum of Naples also has a section on modern art, on the third floor, but you only find out about it when you're there. The first, and still the most important, modern art museum was inaugurated in Rome back in 1883 and houses only Italian works; known with the acronym, GNAM, it also holds temporary exhibitions such as the one on Pre-Raphaelite English artists held in 2011; one of the latest in GNAM was, Secessione e Avanguardia, on Italian art during the decade that preceded WW1, 1905 - 1915, on show between 31 Oct. 2014 and 15 Feb. 2015. In 2002 Rome inaugurated a new contemporary art museum, the MACRO, showcasing 600 works executed during the second half of 20th century by Italian artists. The same year in a brand new building designed by Mario Botta the modern art museum, MART, was inaugurated in Rovereto in the northern region of Trentino-Alto Adige to much acclaim, the building itself is considered a work of modern art. Meanwhile Milan which already had four venues for modern art opened a new one called, Novecento (900), dedicated to 20th-century art, in 2010, actually the collection held on the second floor of Palazzo Ducale was transferred here and expanded by other, new acquisitions and includes paintings by the likes of Picasso, Modigliani, Kandinsky, Matisse, Umberto Boccioni, Giacomo Balla, Giorgio de Chirico and more. Also in 2010 in the Flaminio quarter of Rome a brand new art gallery, MAXXI, opened its gates to modern art lovers; designed by Zaha Hadid MAXXI, as the name implies, displays 21st century artwork. Down in Naples in 2005, the contemporary art museum, PAN, in a modern setting saw the light and exhibits paintings, sculptures, photographs video installations and other contemporary art. What about the Vatican? Well the Vatican Museum in Rome opened a section on modern sacred art back in 1973 and displays religious works by many greats such as: Auguste Rodin, Matisse, Renato Guttuso, Lucio Fontana, Emilio Greco, Paul Gauguin and Marc Chagall.

    In any major Italian town and city, sometimes in really small towns like Lissone, to the north-east of Milan, you come across quality modern art galleries which house a permanent collection or hold temporary exhibitions, the choice for art, from any century, really is limitless in Italy and not many will have the stamina to check out all that's on display however many times they visit the country. In unlikely places like Como where tourists flock to get a glimpse of the famed lake and go on a boat trip, there is also modern art housed in the 17th-century Palazzo Volpi, in the city centre, mostly 20th century art and fine examples from the school of Rationalist art and architecture that took root in 1920s and 1930s in Italy. Also in Como are also held temporary exhibitions in the sumptuous 18th-century, Villa Olmo, the latest was on the theme of Cityscapes showcasing works by artists down the centuries up to contemporary photographers and how they depicted cities.

      Art and meaning can of course be expressed in many ways, how do Italians express themselves in their language, Italian, and what does modern Italian sound like? Ever since Dante et al began using the Tuscan vernacular in their works back in the Middle Ages instead of Latin, how did Italian evolve over the centuries? How popular is Italian as a foreign language? Much more than you would imagine. Meanwhile, remnants of convoluted Latin still survive in modern Italian but interestingly a huge number of English terms have been imported as well over the last 4-5 decades changing the flavour of Italian noticeably, sometimes even dramatically.

SIXTEEN

LANGUAGE MATTERS

If you happen to be an English-speaker you'll find Italian far from easy to learn, coming up against difficult grammar to grasp and challenging pronunciation. Italian derives from Latin, like several other so-called Romance languages such as French, Spanish and Portuguese. English language, though a Germanic tongue, contains a huge number of terms derived from Latin, as much as 60% of the words in a dictionary are of Latin origin. This naturally helps to guess the meaning of a large body of vocabulary when learning Italian, it's easy to guess that 'conversazione' means conversation, and you'll get no prizes for guessing that 'Latino' means Latin. At this point it should be underlined that there are numerous 'false friends' too. Words like 'pretendere' 'attualmente' 'annoiato' 'conveniente' 'libreria' can be interpreted as 'pretend' 'actually' 'annoyed' 'convenient' and 'library' but do they carry the same meaning? Not really, respectively the Italian words stand for: 'to expect' 'currently' 'bored' 'inexpensive' and 'bookshop.' When it comes to creating your own language, putting words into meanings with the correct grammar and/or syntax, things can get complicated, very complicated.

It is often said that Italian is a musical language, this stems from the fact that nearly all words end in a vowel; all musical terms, piano, pianissimo, forte, fortissimo..., are Italian words used unadulterated all over the world. Pronouncing these words as an Italian would is another matter. The most characteristic errors arise from the inability of most English speakers to roll the letter 'r' and tendency to use diphthongs unnecessarily instead of one crisp vowel sound especially when attempting to articulate the vowel that closes the last syllable. The stress is almost always on the last but one syllable, Italian learners get the hang of this quite quickly, sometimes unaware that there are many exceptions e.g. 'chimico' (chemist) has the stress on the first syllable, moving it down to the next syllable would make it sound odd, to say the least; shifting the stress from one syllable to the next may also change the meaning e.g. 'ancora' with the accent on the usual last but one syllable would mean 'still' or 'yet' but if you place the accent on the first syllable it means 'anchor.'

Grammar, sentence structure creates countless problems, Italian nouns, all of them, have genders, OK these also exist in English e.g. manager and manageress, but are very few indeed. There are no logical reasons why a word is considered masculine or feminine, why 'libro' (book) is masculine and 'matita' (pencil) feminine nobody can explain. The gender of the word is easily recognised, those that end in 'o' are masculine and those that end in 'a' are feminine, and to make them plural you just make the 'o' 'i' and 'a' 'e', piece of cake. Then you notice that there are a lot of words that in 'e' in the singular form and you have no idea of their sex. For instance 'bicchiere' (a glass) and confine (border) are 'he' but 'base' (base or basis) and 'fine' (end) are 'she.' There are other more sinister traps, there are words that end in 'a' such as 'problema' or 'panorama' which are actually masculine, there are others that end in 'o' like 'radio' or 'mano' (hand) that are in reality feminine. Is it important to know the gender of the noun? Yes, because the Italian version of the articles, 'a' and 'the' accords with the gender of the word; masculine nouns take 'un', 'il' and 'lo' in the singular and 'una' and 'la' in the feminine cases respectively. The adjective that follows equally accords with the gender, a red car is 'una/la macchina rossa' but a red book is 'un/il libro rosso.' These are just a few examples to highlight the possible complications and are by no means the only ones. For instance if the noun is in plural form, the articles are also plural and the adjectives qualifying too are plural so 'il libro rosso' becomes, 'i libri rossi,' and 'la macchina rossa' becomes le macchine rosse.' Got it?

As in all (I presume) languages Italian too has formal informal forms of address. English speakers by using the plural 'you' needn't worry too much about offending anyone, Italian speakers on the other hand have no such luxury and much care and attention is required to use the informal 'tu' (singular 'you' if you like or as Shakespeare used to say, 'thou') with close friends, children and family but not with strangers or anyone considered worthy of respect. Here it gets tricky, you can't just use the plural 'voi' which corresponds to 'you' instead the third person, singular, feminine form 'lei' is used which stands for 'she' or 'her' (as in 'I like her,' not the possessive in 'her car.' It strangely feels like talking to a third party who is absent, it can get confusing (even for Italians) when you're referring to a feminine person (lei) in the conversation, you really have to point it out to the person you're talking to that it's not 'lei' standing before you but 'lei', say Francesca, e.g. her mother, you were referring to and vice versa. A typical conversation in literal translation would go something like this:

Good morning, how is she/her?
Well, thank you, and she/her?
Very well. How is her mother?
Oh! She is fine.
Where does she live now?
Who me or her?
She/her (here you point your finger to your interlocutor to indicate you're interested in finding out where *she* lives not her mother. Clear?

Fascist dictator Benito Mussolini in 1920s tried to clarify this confusing form of address by making it compulsory to use 'voi' and it did catch on, for a while, over the decades it disappeared remaining only in some parts of southern Italy where still today lei and voi are both used but voi is an extremely formal address used with the elderly and strangers considered worthy of profound deference.

What about the tenses, Italian of course has the present, past and future forms like I presume every language, English certainly, but not necessarily used in the same way. For a start unlike English in Italian verbs are conjugated, for each verb you'll have to learn seven separate words, usually, for example the infinitive parlare (to speak) becomes: io parlo, tu parli, lui/lei/parla, noi parliamo, voi parlate and loro parlano for I, you, he/she, we, you, and they speak respectively but as the verb ending clearly states who is doing the speaking, pronouns are not needed unless you want to emphasise it. Italian present tense is used also for present continuous and future, so 'cosa fai?' literally 'what do you do?' can mean 'what do you do?' but also 'what are you doing?' or 'what are your plans for tomorrow?' by simply adding the word 'domani' (tomorrow), or even in present perfect and present perfect continuous situations like 'vivo a Milano da tre anni' (literally, I live in Italy since three years). Fair enough also English present continuous may be used for future plans and intentions but Italian is far more flexible on this. When it comes to the past tense, here you find some bizarre usage. The simple past, or 'passato remoto' in Italian, is totally ignored in northern Italy, and many parts of central Italy, where the present perfect is widely used instead, also for completed actions in completed times such as 'ho visto Marco ieri' (I have seen Marco yesterday). But not in Tuscany and southern Italy in general where the 'correct' form 'Vidi Marco ieri' (I saw Marco yesterday) is normally used. Written Italian on the other hand uses passato remoto appropriately, novels and poetry would use the past simple in the same way as is used in English. Things get a little more complicated when using the conditional and especially the subjunctive, a little used form in modern English as in, 'if I were you,' or 'they recommended that she be on time.'

Italians use the subjunctive profusely but sometimes get it wrong, as it requires specific verb forms and spelling, and one way to understand somebody's level of education, or language awareness, is taking note of how well they use the subjunctive, or 'congiuntivo' as they say in Italian. Other confusing grammar points include the use of have and be as auxiliaries, in English using a tense like present perfect you say 'she has arrived,' in Italian you have to say 'she is arrived' because with with verbs indicating movement like go, come and arrive, have can't be used, verb to be must be employed instead and if you are caught using have with go that would be substandard Italian and you would risk getting laughed at. Just to confuse this further a verb like 'viaggiare' meaning 'to travel' is clearly a verb that involves moving from one place to another but must be used with the auxiliary have, such is life.

Once you've learnt a bit of Italian, you notice some expressions using numbers but in a way that's odd to an English speaker, for instance when thanking someone an English speaker may say, 'Thanks a million,' an Italian would say, 'Grazie mille' (thanks a thousand), probably they can't think of a situation when that much gratitude needs to be expressed. To explain something briefly they may say, 'Te lo spiego in due parole' (I'll explain in two words); if at a party there were very few people this is expressed by, 'C'erano quattro gatti' (there were four cats); to invite someone for a chat they say, 'Facciamo quattro chiacchere' (let's exchange four pieces of gossip); Sometimes the expression is quite baffling, 'Facciamo due/quattro passi?' (shall we take two/four steps?) to mean go for a short walk; or 'Andiamo a fare due/quattro salti' (shall we take two/four leaps?? to say shall we go dancing; or the truly confusing, 'è successo un 48' (a 48 has happened) to say 'chaos reigned'. The number 48 here refers to 1848 when Italians rebelled against Austrians ruling Northern Italy at the time.

Italy is probably the only country where you can't say, good luck, without almost offending someone or getting a frown.

Straightforward good luck (buona fortuna) is taken to mean the opposite, bringing bad luck instead, Italians, without exception, say, in bocca al lupo, (literally: in the wolf's mouth) this is, probably, referring to the safest place for a wolf's cub to be, naturally one should thank and respond 'grazie' but hardly anyone does, opting for, 'crepi' (let it die) instead, obviously unaware of the hidden meaning, the average Italian wishes the wolf to die! Many dictionaries on the other hand explain it as a hunter's expression coined to ward off malefic, wicked acts, and the wolf is seen as causing such acts by the superstitious, hence 'crepi' would be an appropriate response.

To an English speaker, current Italian usage, especially in formal communication, would sound cluttered, wordy and top heavy with redundant forms. There are many journalists and novelists who write clear, concise prose à la Ernest Hemingway so don't take it as a generalisation, still, official announcements will tend to be far from succinct and sound like legal statements. For instance in TV series a number of products may be advertised by 'naturally' inserting them into some scenes, and the public by law has to be informed of this by passing a message at the bottom of the screen at the start of the programme, it goes: 'Nel programma sono presenti inserimenti di prodotti a fini promozionali' which translates: 'In the programme are present insertions of products for the purpose of promotion.' Groceries and supermarkets usually don't allow pets inside, and a notice is placed at the entrance: 'Al fine della tutela igienico-sanitario degli alimenti, si informa la gentile clientela che i nostri amici animali non sono ammessi all'interno del negozio,' meaning: 'For the purpose of safeguarding health related hygiene of food items on display, clients are warned that our animal friends are not allowed inside the store.'

Bureaucratic language is packed with not only redundant forms but also archaic vocabulary. Common terms such as nome (name), firmare (sign) avviare (start up) malattia (illness), pagamento (payment), cambiare (to change) in bureaucratese become: nominativo (nominative), sottoscrivere (underwrite), dare corso (give course), evento morboso (morbid event), corresponsione (corresponding amount) and apportare modifiche (generate change). Much effort goes into 'refining' the language, rather than saying corruption you get 'comportamento corruttivo' (corruptive behaviour), blind becomes 'non vedente' (non-seer), disabled is 'diversamento abile' (differently able). Linguists are well aware of this and effort has been made in recent years, courses have been held to use plain Italian but as the saying goes, old habits die hard.

In recent years everyday Italian has changed, one outstanding change immediately noticeable to those who have spent a few years in the country is the need to emphasize, a simple 'yes' or 'no' or 'ciao' even the superlative praise 'the best' are not seen enough and are further highlighted by the use of assolutamente (absolutely) so we get 'assolutamente sì' 'assolutamente no' 'la migliore in assoluto' (absolutely the best) and ciao, which is used both to say hi/hello and bye, when used to say 'bye' also on the phone, is repeated several times, 'ciao, ciao, ciao, ciao, ciao...' as if the person on the receiving end is distracted, preoccupied or perhaps the signal is bad, or something and may not have heard it.

How many people speak Italian worldwide and how popular is it as a second language to learn? Apart from the 60.5 million or so Italians, the southern Swiss Canton of Ticino, parts of Canton Grisons, Istria Region of Slovenia, Istria County of Croatia also speak Italian as a native tongue. According to a 2012 study by Eurobarometer, commissioned by the EU, there are around 14 million Italian speakers in the EU. To this must be added the Italian diaspora living in the Americas, as well as in the business circles of Tunisia, pockets of Albania, Monaco, and the former Italian colonies Eritrea, Ethiopia and Somalia where Italian is still popular bringing the total number of speakers, including Italy, to around 85 million worldwide. In the list of most widely spoken languages drawn by UNESCO, Italian comes 18th, Mandarin Chinese, English and Spanish taking the first positions but currently popularity of Italian as a second language places it much higher; the figures released by the Italian Foreign Ministry in Oct 2014 is indeed encouraging; currently some 1.5 million students are busy learning Italian making it the fourth or fifth most popular foreign language according to the Ministry.

Among the Romance languages, Italian is the nearest to Latin which as a language continued being spoken many centuries after the demise of Roman Empire in 5th century AD. A vernacular known as Vulgar Latin meanwhile took hold among the ordinary people. The earliest written record of Vulgar Latin, a four-line riddle, was discovered in Verona in 1924 and aptly called, the Veronese Riddle, dated 8th or early 9th century. Then came the so called, Placiti Cassinesi, legal documents regarding a dispute between Benedictine monasteries and a local landowner in the Monte Cassini province in southern Italy and were recognised as first examples of vernacular Italian that would be used by the Tuscan poet Dante Alighieri in the 14th century when penning his epic poem, Divina Commedia. The language used by Italy's supreme poet aimed to make his writings comprehensible to a much wider section of the population, not only the educated elite still using Latin.

Only in 1861 when Italy was united as one country thanks to efforts of Giuseppe Garibalbi and Camillo Benso Cavour, was the Tuscan vernacular adopted as the national language. Ironically, Cavour, the able statesman behind the unification, spoke poor Italian, like many of his countrymen in Piemonte at the time, expressing himself best in French. However, down the centuries Italy's cities were like states and these city-states had their own local idioms, these dialects continued to be used well after the unification, and are still not exactly dead. According to statistics released by ISTAT between 1995 and 2012 only around 53% of Italians spoke standard Italian at home, 56% did it with friends and 85% used it when talking with strangers, the remaining percentage spoke the local dialect. The spread of standardised Italian took hold with the arrival of TV. Starting mid 1950s, Italian TV programmes and specific language lessons were broadcast in standard Italian helping the nation to communicate with one tongue. The same ISTAT figures also pointed out the use of dialect was declining and its place taken over by foreign language learning, 32% of the 25-44 age group declared that they knew a second language, mostly English.

Ever since 1950s Italian language has had a love affair with English/American terminology and has been importing words into Italian in massive doses. I've dealt with this in detail in my earlier book, 25 Years in Italy, re-published in 2017, and won't repeat the same content here. Suffice to say that the phenomenon is still in course and the mass media keeps using English terms at the cost of often confusing the general public who may not be well versed in English. Is the government concerned with this disrespect for Italian? Not really politicians are actually among the worst offenders. Starting 2013 expressions like 'jobs act' (employment reform package), 'spending review' (searching for ways to reduce state spending), 'zoning' (allocating specific areas for prostitution), 'local tax,' 'green growth,' 'covered bonds,' 'quantitative easing' (of national debt) and many others have been freely used by politicians, journalists and commentators.

Italy's business community is among the top English terminology importers, new expressions turn up every day. We go from 'crisis opportunity,' 'insider trading,' 'fundraising,' 'outsourcing,' 'export specialist,' to 'transfer pricing,' 'brand premium' and 'flagship store.' The tourist trade serves us expressions like 'wedding tourism,' 'unfair' (practices), 'all inclusive' and 'low cost.' More general terms that have come to dominate recently include the ever present: 'social network' 'selfie' 'smoke free' 'gluten free' 'vegan day' 'wedding planner' 'appeal' 'location' 'work in progress' and 'Italian sounding' referring to foreign food products pretending to have an Italian association.

It would be wrong to say that nobody is concerned with this language invasion, often readers, viewers and social media patrons protest this linguistic overkill giving Italian versions of these foreign terms perfectly comprehensible to all, why say 'spending review' when you can say, 'revisione dei conti' or why say 'wedding planner' when you can say 'organizzatore dei matrimoni?' The answer is simple really, the English version sounds much more sophisticated, modern and hip, alas. Notices in English are sometimes put up to inform, or instruct the foreigners, or tourists, but more often than not there are errors in them, at a car park in a village facing Lake Como, I saw this: 'In yellow lines classified to residents authorised.' I guessed that they meant parking spots with yellow borders are for residents only. In Como I see this, 'Car Washing' advertising a car wash. I frequently see this: 'Don't walk on grass' or 'Don't touch' no please or a little more courteous form is used. In Italy they really don't want you to walk on grass anywhere and warn you at every opportunity to keep off. Visiting a villa and beautiful gardens on the shores of Lake Maggiore, they cut it short and ungrammatically posted several signs: 'Forbidden walk grass.'

What about Italy's pop music? Do singers, song writers use English lyrics in place of the local language, some do but let's see what Italy's popular music scene is like these days. The best way to get a glimpse of this fascinating world is really to visit Sanremo Music Festival which every February showcases the best of the nation's current and future talent, winning a prize at Sanremo is not unlike winning an Oscar, it gives a big push to new singers to launch their careers.

SEVENTEEN

SANREMO...AND MORE

There are few events that capture more media attention than the Sanremo music festival that kicks off in February sometime and manages to attract a huge number of viewers who tune in to state TV channel, RAI 1, that airs this annual song contest to watch the show and discover the new voices in Italian pop music. Virtually all well-known Italian singers, many of them also songwriters, made it big by participating in Sanremo and winning a prize. Competition is thus fierce, controversy before, during and after never ending. All aspects of the event with the official title, Festival della Canzone Italiana di Sanremo, are covered in detail not only the quality of songs but also how much the event costs the tax payer, the new rules which may be introduced, the host(s), guests from abroad, their pay, all sorts of gossip concerning the participants, and especially the audience share.

The 2015, 2016 and 2017 editions were no different, veteran TV host, Carlo Conti, a fifty something, bespectacled Tuscan with a permanent tan, took over from slightly younger Fabio Fazio (Italy's answer to David Letterman) who'd run the show for the previous two years together with highly popular stand-up comedian/actress, Luciana Littizzetto (a former music teacher). The event which gathers momentum starting December was set to be different from Fazio's version when 16 big names, 'Campioni' (champions) participated, Conti announced he'd increase that to 20 bearing in mind the quality and quantity songs that every year inundate the selection committee. Along with these Campioni, or former winners, newcomers also participate after all this is a celebration of contemporary Italian music but also a sort of talent show that aims to discover new singers, alas only eight newcomers took part, the same as with Fazio. Over five evenings via a process of elimination a winner in each of the two categories i.e. Campioni and Nuove Proposte (new singers, aged 16 - 36) are finally announced. Who decides the winners? Up to the semi-final stage 50% of the vote comes from a jury made up of professional musicians, the remaining 50% is decided by the public who vote for their favourites by sending a text message. Starting the semifinals, fourth evening, 40% of the vote comes from the professional jury, 30% from the public and 30% from a jury made up of the general public. Fazio had asked each contestant to bring along two songs, Conti insisted on one song each but introduced a new section, the contestants had to sing a cover as well on the third evening. He also decided to give more visibility to the Nuove Proposte by bringing them on during prime-time rather than late when audience share tends to go down.

In the 2017 edition the winner in the Campioni category was the 34-year-old Francesco Gabbani (born in the Tuscan city of Carrara) with a catchy tune called, Occidentali's Karma, and represented Italy at the Eurovision Song Contest 2017 attracting enough votes to conquer a respectable 6th position. The runner-up was Fiorella Mannoia, a former stuntwoman born in Rome, participating for the fifth time. In the newcomers category the jury voted 20-year-old Lele (real name Raffaelel Esposito), from Naples, the winner; the runner-up was Maldestro (real name Antonio Prestieri), also from Naples born in 1985, an amazing number of contemporary Italian singers use just one name obviously trying to sound more hip or even mysterious.

Sanremo song contest, music festival began in 1951 to celebrate contemporary Italian music and the very first edition was won by Nilla Pizzi (1919 - 2011) from Bologna with a song called, Grazie dei fiori (thanks for the flowers). It is held in the township of Sanremo situated in the Liguria region. To this day a special commission screens and finally selects the songs that will be performed, this procedure takes months, the composer has to be an

Italian and the song has to have Italian lyrics; this rule continued till 1981 when a few singers were allowed to sing in English, and one in French, after 1984 this rule was abandoned; however during 1960s some foreign singers were allowed to take part in the main competition singing in Italian with 'funny' British/American accents and also partly or totally in English. Linguistic flexibility has continued to this day. The winning song was sent to Eurovision Song Contest, set up in 1956 apparently inspired by Sanremo, to represent Italy. For an Italian singer, winning the Leone (lion) di Sanremo is considered the most prestigious achievement. Three new prizes have been introduced since then, the Premio della Critica (critics' award) in 1982 now named after the first winner of this prize, Mia Martini, the Nuove Proposte in 1984 to discover new, young singers and in recent years the Premio Volare (after the hugely famous song, Volare by Domenico Modugno, the winner in 1958) for best lyrics. Sanremo was broadcast on TV for the first time in 1955 till then it was only listened to on the radio. Today it is televised in Eurovision and millions tune in also from abroad to follow the event.

Ten most recent Sanremo winners in the Campioni category

2017 - Francesco Gabbani - *Occidentali's karma*

2016 - Stadio - *Un giorno mi dirai*

2015 - Il Volo (P. Barone, I. Boschetto and G. Ginoble) - *Grande amore*

2014 Arisa - *Controvento*

2013 Marco Mengoni - *L'essenziale*

2012 Emma - *Non è l'inferno*

2011 Roberto Vecchioni - *Chiamami ancora amore*

2010 Valerio Scanu - *Per tutte le volte che...*

2009 Marco Carta - *La forza mia*

2008 Giò di Tonno and Lola Ponce - *Colpo di fulmine*

2007 Simone Cristicchi - *Ti regalerò una rosa*

Ten most recent Sanremo winners in the Nuove Proposte category

2017 Lele - *Oramai*

2016 Francesco Gabbani - *Amen*

2015 Giovanni Caccamo - *Ritornerò da Te*

2014 Rocco Hunt - *Nu juorno buono*

2013 Antonio Maggio - *Mi servirebbe sapere*

2012 Alessandro Casillo - *È vero (che ci sei)*

2011 Raphael Gualazzi - *Follia d'amore*

2010 Tony Maiello - *Il linguaggio della resa*

2009 Arisa - *Sincerità*

2008 Sonohra - *L'amore*

  A lot of people watch the show but exactly what percentage of TV viewers it attracts began to be measured in 1987 with veteran presenter Pippo Baudo running the show, amazingly it clocked up nearly 69% of the share, just under 16 million viewers. Baudo hosted the festival numerous times and in 1995 he improved on 1987 when over 16.8 million tuned in, a record that hasn't been broken yet. Fazio in 2014 managed around 8.8 million with 39% of the share. Carlo Conti's 2015 edition kicked off with Chiara Galiazzo singing, *Straordinario*. Guest stars, Al Bano and

Romina Power caused a bit of a stir when they once again sang together 24 years after their last participation. They used to be hugely popular as husband and wife performing as a duo, until they got divorced; Al Bano carried on solo and have enjoyed much success with his characteristic high pitched voice worthy of a tenor. The couple sang a medley of their most catchy tunes receiving a big applause. High profile guests Conti invited include Hollywood stars Charlize Theron and Will Smith, the British band, Spandau Ballet immensely popular in 1980s, the 24-year-old, hugely popular Ed Sheeran also from UK, Italian rock star Gianna Nannini, Pop music idols, Tiziano Ferro, Biagio Antonacci and for some reason Mr and Mrs Anania, a couple from southern Italy and their 16 children, the largest family in Italy, who filled the spacious stage easily. How successful was the show? The opening night in 2015 went well obtaining nearly 50% of the share. The following four night were equally upbeat in terms of shares averaging 48.6%, the final night had a record 54.2% audience share or 11.84 million viewers making it the most successful over the last 10 years. Who won? In the newcomers category 25-year-old Sicilian, Giovanni Caccamo, came first with the romantic song, Ritornerò da Te, in the Campioni section the trio, Piero Barone, Ignazio Boschetto and Gianluca Ginoble, calling themselves, Il Volo, won the top award with another romantic song, Grande Amore. In case you're wondering, Malika Ayane came second, and Nek, third. Conti's 2016 and 2017 editions were equally successful attracting over 50% of the share.

Here are the 22 songs, and singers, that took part in the Campioni category, 2017

Di rose e di spine - Al Bano

Tutta colpa mia - Elodie

Fatti bella per te - Paola Turci

Vedrai - Samuel

Che sia benedetta - Fiorella Mannoia

Do retta a te - Nesli and Alice Paba

Il diario degli errori - Michele Bravi

Portami via - Fabrizio Moro

Fatalmente male - Giusy Ferreri

La prima stella - Gigi D'Alessio

Togliamoci la voglia - Raige and Giulia Luzi

L'ottava meraviglia - Ron

Vietata morire - Ermal Meta

Mani nelle mani - Michele Zarillo

Il cielo non mi basta - Lodovica Comello

Con te - Sergio Sylvestre

Ragazzi fuori - Clementino

Nel mezzo di un applauso - Alessio Bernabei

Nessun posto è casa mia - Chiara Galiazzo

Occidentali's karma - - Francesco Gabbani

Ora esisti solo tu - Bainca Atzei

Spostato di un secondo - Marco Masini

Here are the eight songs, and singers, that took part in the Nuove Proposte category, 2017

Ciò che resta - Leonardo Lamacchia

Cose che danno ansia - Tommaso Pini

Canzone per Federica - Maldestro

Le canzoni fanno male - Marianne Mirage

Oramai - Lele

Universo - Francesco Guasti

Insieme - Valeria Farinacci

Nel mare ci sono i coccodrilli - Federico Braschi

How much does Sanremo cost to the taxpayers bearing in mind it's the state TV RAI organising the event and footing the bill. Despite all the media coverage, razzmatazz, high audience share and hence lots of advertising revenue, Sanremo did not generate income for RAI up until the 2014 edition when a small profit was announced, it regularly lost money, in the three editions 2011, 2012, 2013, a total of €20.1 million of losses were announced, that's €1.34 million per night of the 15 nights that it was aired despite substantial cuts had been introduced regarding production costs and payments to guests stars, it remained a loss making exercise; glamorous and glittery but loss making just the same. Come Carlo Conti to everyone's amazement Sanremo actually made a profit of some €6 million in 2015 and repeated the success also for 2016. In case you're wondering, Carlo Conti earned €500,000 for running the show in 2015, and €550,000 in 2016, that's on top of his annual salary of €1.3 million. Fazio the year before was earning €600,000 on top of his annual pay of €1.8 million from RAI, and for the 2011, 2012 editions singer/songwriter Gianni Morandi was paid €800,000 to host the event each time. Considering that some three million fewer viewers tuned in to watch Sanremo in 2014 with respect to 2013, RAI's balance books didn't improve. Conti's edition however did cost less judging for instance by his lower fee and the substantial increase in audience share leading to a the €6 million profit mentioned above. The great singer-songwriter Claudio Baglioni will be hosting Sanremo in 2018, good luck to him.

Is Sanremo the only talent show in town? No, it isn't, there are others most popular of which are Italian versions of X-Factor and The Voice. The former aired by Sky TV reached its 11th edition in 2017 and has been attracting increasing number of viewers, the latter, launched in 2013 is hosted by the state TV RAI 2. The winner of X-Factor in 2017 was the 25-year-old Sicilian, Lorenzo Licitra, dubbed 'Italian Bubblè' by the Italian mass media. Unlike Sanremo X-Factor doesn't mind the contestants singing in English. The runner-up was the band called, Maneskin, led by 18-yearl-old Damiano David of Rome. The Voice on the other hand made headlines around the world when a nun called, Suor Cristina won in 2014 becoming an overnight sensation with the world media, millions listened to her winning, upbeat pop song, Lungo La Riva. The music-loving nun announced in a TV interview that she'd really like to sing Madonna's hit single, Like a Virgin. The 2016 edition was won by Alice Paba with runner-up Charles Kaplan, the programme did not air in 2017 but is returning in 2018 with Al Bano as main host.

All-Time Best-Selling 25 Songs in Italy

1) *Questo Piccolo Grande Amore* - Claudio Baglioni
2) *Vita Spericolata* - Vasco Rossi
3) *Azzurro* - Adriano Calentano (Paolo Conte)
4) *Stayin' Alive* - Bee Gees

5) *E Poi* - Mina
6) *Grande Grande Grande* - Mina
7) *I Giardini di Marzo* - Lucio Battisti
8) *E Tu...* - Claudio Baglioni
9) *Tunnel of Love* - Dire Straits
10) *Il Cielo in una Stanza* - Gino Paoli (and Mina)
11) *A Chi* - Fausto Leali
12) *Amor Mio* - Lucio Battisti (and Mina)
13) *A Whiter Shade of Pale* - Procol Harum
14) *Another Brick in the Wall* - Pink Floyd
15) *Let It Be* - Beatles
16) *29 Settembre* - Lucio Battisti
17) *Bang Bang* - Cher and Equipe 84
18) *Ancora Tu* - Lucio Battisti
19) *Amico* - Renato Zero
20) *Il Padrino* - Santo and Johnny
21) *Nel Blu Dipinto di Blu (Volare)* - Domenico Modugno
22) *La Nostra Favola* - Jimmy Fontana
23) *Yesterday* - Beatles
24) *Emozioni* - Lucio Battisti
25) *Only You* - Platters

Of the 15 Italians in the above list, all except Lucio Battisti (1943-1998), are still working, still making music.

Now that we've seen where Italian pop music stands, who the most popular singers, songwriters are, let's take a look at what the classical music scene is like in particular opera, an Italian invention.

EIGHTEEN

ITALIAN OPERA

The history of opera is fascinating. It began in Florence in 1589 at the wedding of Tuscany's Grand Duke Ferdinand de Medici's marriage to French Princess Christine of Lorraine. The duke asked the numerous gifted poets, musicians and artists he patronised to devise something spectacular to impress the nobles, aristocrats and the powerful, he wanted the news of this Tuscany-France alliance to be noted and remarked. They came up with 'intermedi' which as the name implies were to be entertainment in the middle of another entertainment, usually a play, a tournament perhaps or even a feast. The main amusement at the wedding was a long, 5-act play, La Pellegrina (The Pilgrim) by Girolamo Bargagli, hence six intermedi were needed one at the beginning, four between the acts and one at the end to wrap up. Bernardo Buontalenti, a leading artist in Florence, spent eight months designing costumes, and scenery, and equipped the Uffizi Theatre with platforms, flying machines, pulleys, props and more to amaze the audience with a series of special effects including storms, destruction and dragons; the music was catchy and upbeat, the performers enacted mythological stories while dancing, singing virtuoso solos or in chorus that held the attention of the audience trying hard not to fall asleep watching Bargagli's lengthy drama. The duke was so pleased, with the intermedi that is, that he had them repeated over the following days and had the music and lyrics published, one reason they've survived to this day.

Intermedi, however, were not opera, the stories they contained were told statically, no drama was conveyed. The idea of putting music to drama was already a main topic of conversation among the intellectuals, musicians, artists and poets in Florence who formed a society called Accademia degli Alterati in 1569 aiming to improve the cultural standing of their members through mastery of proper social conduct, elegant speech and knowledge of all the arts and sciences. Amongst many other cultural issues, they were intrigued by the ancient Greek dramas and were convinced that these tragedies were written more for singing than speaking. This was probably true, at least part of the play was sung bearing in mind the word orchestra derives from Greek and meant the semicircular area in front of the stage where the chorus sang. Script alone, however well-written, they were convinced couldn't express drama with the same emotional engagement as musical, sung delivery. Under the guidance of wealthy merchant Jacopo Corsi, who was also a harpsichord player and composer, Florentine musicians Jacopo Peri and Giulio Caccini as well as the renowned poet Ottavio Rinuccini joined forces but were soon faced with a major obstacle, at the time polyphonic music was all the rage, played in various keys, many sounds came together to produce an overall pleasant effect, this was unsuitable for reciting words to music as the Corsi's group, called Camerata, intended. Music had to be simplified, to allow the utterance of words halfway between singing and speaking i.e. recitative acting. Camerata member Vincenzo Galilei (the father of famous Galileo, the astronomer), a music theorist and composer, is credited as the discoverer of a new style of monodic music which could accompany the actor-singer to give more dramatic power to his words. Alas, Galilei passed away in 1591, seven years too early to see the performance of the first opera in history. In 1592, practical steps were taken to create, *dramma per musica*, the earliest moniker for opera. Applying Galilei's ideas, Peri wrote the music to Rinuccini's poem, Dafne (Daphne), and finally using the recitative style Dafne was performed at Corsi's house in Florence in February 1598.

Hence an art form where art, literature, music, acting and singing come together to delight the senses was thus born and became richer and richer as time went. A substantial improvement, a turning point, was made as early as 1607 with Cremona-born composer Claudio Monteverdi who staged, La Favola d'Orfeo (The Legend of Orpheus), in Mantua to please his patron, Duke Vincenzo Gonzaga. Monteverdi used 38 instruments (including modern violins invented by his fellow violin-makers in Cremona), a chorus, ballet dancers and eleven principal singers led by tenor, Francesco Rasi. Compared to spectacular Orfeo, Peri's Dafne, and Euridice staged in 1600, seemed feeble efforts. With Monteverdi, opera became a composer's medium that soon infected many other composers in Italy and abroad delighting music lovers all over the world to this day. For those unfamiliar with operas, they invariably start with a powerful, catchy overture, the recitative acting is punctuated with melodious songs called arias that eventually become all-time classics, the most memorable parts of any opera, and linger on forever.

The first Italian opera to be performed abroad was Galatea, author unknown, in Warsaw in 1828. Shortly after La Liberazione Di Ruggiero by Francesca Caccini (1587 - circa1641) was also staged there and is considered the first opera to be composed by a woman. Over the next three centuries or so, numerous musicians composed operas each in his or her own language but the appeal of Italian must have been strong, a number of foreign musicians composed operas in Italian too including Georg F. Handel, Christoph F. Gluck, Czech musician Josef Myslievecek and most famous of them all Mozart who wrote some of the most memorable operas in history in Italian: Le Nozze di Figaro (The Marriage of Figaro), Don Giovanni, Così Fan Tutte and Idomeneo.

At first the composers took all the merit, and applause, for an opera's success, in time the performers began sharing the spot light and eventually many became stars even superstars. Neapolitan Enrico Caruso (1873 - 1921) was an international star, Beniamino Gigli (1890 - 1957) was another. In 1950s Maria Callas (1923 - 1977), Magda Olivero (1910 - 2014), and Rosanna Carteri, were famous sopranos singing with male counterparts like Mario

Del Monaco and Giuseppe Di Stefano. Spain's Placido Domingo and José Carreras were no less famous starting 1960s, Italy's Luciano Pavarotti (1935 - 2007) was a megastar, his place would be hard to fill but 1958-born Andrea Boccelli is considered his musical heir. Pavarotti, Carreras and Domingo performed as Three Tenors around the world obtaining huge success everywhere. Meanwhile a brand new generation of opera singers are filling the theatres these days, from Italy the threesome, Piero Barone, Ignazio Boschetto and Gianluca Ginoble, still in their twenties, are already international stars enjoying the same success as the Three Tenors did before the young singers had even been born.

Right from the beginning understanding what was being sung on stage has been difficult, even for those who know the language the opera is performed in. In the case of singing Italian operas for non-Italians has been a problem, the professional singers undoubtedly did their homework and learnt at least the words they were uttering, others learnt Italian, but still the less than perfect pronunciation has always created further comprehension difficulties. The same of course goes for Italian tenors, sopranos etc singing in languages other than Italian. To understand the dialogues, and follow the story one had to buy a libretto and read it before or during the performance. To overcome this difficulty Lotfi Mansouri, the director of Canadian Opera Company, introduced what's known as surtitles (aka supertitles), as opposed to subtitles, in 1983, so that the audience could follow the dialogue in Richard Strauss's Elektra. New York City Opera the same year also used surtitles, this method has now spread virtually everywhere. In Milan's La Scala instead of surtitles you can follow the dialogue on the back of the seat before you a bit like watching a movie on a plane. In the case of an outdoor event like in Verona's Opera Festival, the only solution is either to be familiar with the story, or get hold of a libretto, a vendor tends to pass by before the opera starts so that anyone interested can purchase a copy.

Italy, as the inventor of the genre, has produced numerous opera composers down the centuries and many of these gifted musicians still enjoy immense popularity today. According to the online source, operabase.com, which lists all opera productions and performances around the world as well as giving information on individual composers and singers, of the 42 most popular composers considered for the five opera seasons from 2011 to 2016, 8 Italians made the list:

1. Giuseppe Verdi (1813 - 1901) - 3,728 productions worldwide
2. Giacomo Puccini (1858 - 1924) - 2,597

3. Gioachino Rossini (1792 - 1868) - 1,197

4. Gaetano Donizetti (1797 - 1848) - 1,103

5. Vincenzo Bellini (1801 - 1835) - 289

6. Ruggero Leoncavallo (1857 - 1919) - 259

7. Pietro Mascagni (1863 - 1945) - 235

8. Claudio Monteverdi (1567 - 1643) - 149

If we were to look at the most frequently staged Italian operas around the world between 2011 and 2016, including Italy, works of just four composers, Verdi, Puccini, Rossini and Donizetti occupy the top 10 positions:

1. Traviata - Verdi - 869 productions

2. La Boheme - Puccini - 672

3. Tosca - Puccini - 608

4. Madama Butterfly - Puccini - 634

5. Il Barbiere di Siviglia - Rossini - 591

6. Rigoletto - Verdi - 523

7. Aida - Verdi - 392

8. L'elisir d'amore - Donizetti - 378

9. Nabucco - Verdi - 314

10. Turandot - Puccini - 255

There are of course numerous non-Italian composers too like the giants Mozart and Wagner; despite the competition, in the top 10 most frequently staged composers over the five seasons starting 2011, there were four Italians, here's the full list:

1. Verdi - 3,728 productions ; 16,265 performances

2. Mozart - 2,480; 11,860

3. Puccini - 2,597; 11,494

4. Rossini - 1,197; 5,070

5. Wagner - 1,219; 4,456

6. Donizetti - 1,103; 4,393

7. Bizet - 807; 3,710

8. J. Strauss - 520; 2,934

9. Tchaikovsky - 616; 2,541

10. R. Strauss - 499; 2,302

Needless to say huge numbers of people attend opera, when the opera season in Milan's La Scala, often quoted as the most prestigious opera house in the world, opens on December 7th, it is a major event, which, in recent years has been broadcast live around the world, people dress up and go to the cinema to watch the musical drama unfold. Every sizeable town let alone major city in Italy has a historical theatre most of them dating back to 18th or 19th century. Unfortunately these beautiful buildings have nearly all been struck by fire and had to be rebuilt, most recent examples are the Fenice of Venice and Petruzzelli in Bari. La Scala on the other hand had a major restoration done. Here are Italy's top 10 opera houses:

1. Teatro Alla Scala - Milan

2. Teatro San Carlo - Naples

3. Teatro La Fenice - Venice

4. Teatro del Maggio Musicale Fiorentino - Florence

5. Teatro Regio Torino - Turin

6. Teatro Comunale di Bologna

7. Teatro Dell'Opera - Rome

8. Teatro Massimo - Palermo

9. Teatro Verdi - Pisa

10. Teatro Verdi - Parma

The above list doesn't of course include the summer opera festivals around Italy most famous of which is held at the Roman amphitheatre, Arena, in Verona; in Rome the 1800-year-old Caracalla Baths complex doubles as a venue for al fresco opera; Puccini Opera Festival at Torre del Lago, near Lucca where Puccini was born, and Rossini Opera Festival in Pesaro, the great composer's native city, also draw big crowds. Unsurprisingly the birth places of all composers of note have a theatre or festival of sorts devoted to them, in Bergamo where Donizetti was born is a theatre named after him, in the small town of Jesi, in Le Marche region, there's a theatre named after Pergolesi and his music is kept alive in honour of the town's most famous son. Verdi was born in a hamlet called Roncole in the outskirts of Busseto, a township in the province of Parma and the main theatre in Parma is better known as Teatro Verdi.

How do Italy's opera houses compare with the best around the world? Quite well, as there are two of them in the top 10 opera houses listed by National Geographic:

1. La Scala - Milan

2. Teatro San Carlo - Naples

3. Teatro Colon - Buenos Aires, Argentina

4. The Royal Opera House - London Valtinoni

5. The Bolshoi - Moscow

6. Sydney Opera House

7. Paris Opéra

8. Opéra Royal - Versailles, France

9. Vienna Staatsoper - Austria

10. Metropolitan - New York

Although their works are much less frequently staged, there are also living Italian opera composers. The 10 most successful, judging by the number of their operas produced across the world over the five seasons 2009 and 2014, include two ladies:

1. Salvatore Sciarrino (b.1947) - 22 productions (82 performances)

2. Luca Francesconi (b.1956) - 8 (27)

3. Pierangelo Valtinoni (b.1959) - 6 (51)

4. Giorgio Battistelli (b. 1953) - 6 (22)

5. Marco Tutino (b.1954) - 6 (18)

6. Lucia Ronchetti (b.1963) - 5 (24)

7. Lorenzo Ferrero (b.1951) - 4 (18)

8. Oscar Bianchi (b.1975) - 4 (13)

9. Marco Betta (b.1964) - 3 (15)

10. Silvia Colasanti (b.1975) - 3 (9)

How do these gifted musicians compare with non-Italian, living composers? The top three places in terms of number of works produced over the five seasons starting 2009, were not Italians, the most popular was composer Philip Glass (b.1937) from USA with 79 productions, the runner-up was another American, Jake Heggie (b.1951) with 29 productions and the third, Peter Maxwell Davies (b.1934) from UK with 27. The only Italian in the top 10 was Sciarrino, placed 8th, with 22 productions.

Over the 2011 -2016 season, of the 40 most popular living composers considered, only two Italians made the list: Salvatore Sciarrini, placed 10th with 25 productions and 86 performances, and Pierangelo Valtinoni, placed 36th with 7 productions and 25 performances of his works. American composers Glass and Heggie again occupied the first two positions with Germany's Peter Lund coming third.

Opera is not only a cultural event in Italy, it is also a tourist attraction, tens of 1000s fly in to attend the Verona Opera Festival in summer, or Maggio Musicale Fiorentino in May in Florence, or perhaps a premiere at La Scala or San Carlo in Naples. To carry these opera lovers the national carrier, Alitalia, used to put on extra flights, this job or air transport has now been taken over by low-cost airlines such as Easy Jet and Ryan Air. What's happened to Alitalia? It's still flying but is only half Italian, you can read the details of Alitalia's story in the next chapter.

NINETEEN

ALITALIA TAKES OFF...SORT OF

Italy's national carrier began 2015 a little less national, as of Jan 1st, 2015, it was half owned by Etihad Airlines of Abu Dhabi, actually with 51% of the shares it is still controlled by Italians but only just and if it hadn't been for Etihad it would certainly have gone bankrupt and faded into history; between 2008 and the deal with Etihad, Alitalia had lost some €1.6 billion. How did this economic disaster come to be and how it was handled is an interesting example of how Italians go out of their way, whatever the cost, to keep Italian companies Italian.

      Alitalia was born in Sep 1946. The first Alitalia flight took off on May 5th, 1947 and flew from Turin to Rome and on to Catania, the plane used for this historic undertaking was a three-engine Fiat G-12 E. The same year in July the very first international flight of Alitalia carried 38 passengers from Rome to Oslo in a Savoia Marchetti SM95. It's interesting to note that both planes were made in Italy. In 1950 four-engine DC4 planes made in USA began serving Alitalia by that time snacks were replaced by hot meals and wine, Italians served good quality of each attracting international travellers who enjoyed these extras. In 1957, Alitalia-Linee Aeree Italiane, was created, the new, bigger company employed 3,000, owned 37 planes and extended its routes, and was hence able to compete with other major airlines, it swiftly moved from 20th to 12th largest carrier in the world. Just as well, in 1960, Olympic games were held in Rome and Alitalia was the official airline flying huge numbers of passengers to the event, for the first time it flew over a million people in and out of Italy. Rome's main airport, Leonardo da Vinci (Fiumicino) was inaugurated and the first jet planes purchased.

By 1970 Alitalia displayed a new logo on its planes, the characteristic A in the national colour green, white and red, replaced the winged arrow, it became the first carrier to fly only jet planes, Boeing 747 Jumbos came into service and passenger and cargo traffic especially to North America dramatically increased. Early 1980s the company began buying new planes, large capacity Airbus 300 and MD Super 80 models, which were used for short to mid-range flights, whereas long haul flights were handled by Boeing's flexible B747 Combis that could carry both passengers and cargo. At the beginning of 1990s MD 11s with their high-tech instrumentation and control panels made their appearance, they could fly for 12,000 km without refuelling. Alitalia employees' uniforms got a new look, Giorgio Armani saw to it, the 1,000-mile programme was introduced to give frequent fliers incentive to continue using Alitalia. In 2001 the airline joined Sky Team Alliance along with Air France, Delta Air, Korean Air, Aeromexico and CSA Czech Airlines. More modern and efficient Boeing B777 replaced B747s for long-distance flights. In 1995 Alitalia acquired Air One to serve domestic destinations at low cost. The lucrative Milan-Rome route was only served with Alitalia and Air One up to 2013.

In Jan. 2009 ailing Alitalia unable to compete with low cost airlines, despite Air One, was privatised for the first time in its history, the new company was called Alitalia CAI (Compagnia Aerea Italiana) and was floated on the stock exchange. A closer look at the stock holders reveal around 20% of the shares were held by Poste Italiane (Italian Post) 65% of which is owned by Italian Ministry of Economy and Finance, the remaining 35% is owned by a savings/lending bank called Cassa di Depositi e Prestiti which is 70% owned by the Italian Treasury! Most of the other share holders were Italian too.

The steps that preceded this patriotic move to keep the new Alitalia Italian is a good example of how blind, or apparent, patriotism can lead to economic disaster. By 2008 Alitalia had accumulated a huge debt of €3 billion, Air France made a bid to take over Alitalia and even offered to pay €1.4 billion of this debt but an industrial plan studied to make the deal feasible meant laying off 2,100 Alitalia employees and transforming Rome's Fiumicino into a hub and reducing the capacity of Milan's Malpensa. Italy's three main trade unions, CGIL, UIL, and CISL, refused to accept, even if relatively generous compensation was offered for these employees. Industrial action, demonstrations in Rome ensued. Lega Nord joined the protest vociferously, Malpensa cannot be sacrificed they insisted. The main opposition party leader, Silvio Berlusconi, gearing up for the imminent general elections in April 2008, in coalition with Lega Nord, heavily campaigned against the sale of Alitalia to the French, he truly went out of his way to find 'suitable' Italian investors to take control of the national carrier. Berlusconi's party won the elections, refused Air France's offer and managed to find a group of Italian investors headed by Roberto Colaninno willing to take over Alitalia on condition that its entire debt was paid by the government. A Golden, and Bad Company, were hence created, Italian taxpayers footed the bill and paid for the debt, Colaninno's group took the helms of Alitalia CAI promising to create a profit making airline in the near future. Over the following six years Alitalia nearly bled to death accumulating debts worth €1.6 billion. A buyer/partner was urgently needed, the owners of Etihad Airlines of Abu Dhabi made an offer.

     Alas, Etihad's offer was similar to that of Air France, 2,170 employees would have to be dismissed, Rome would have to be the main hub and loss-making Air One would cease to exist to help reduce costs and unlike other major airline companies such as Lufthansa, Air France-KLM and Iberia, it would no longer have a low-cost carrier. The new airline, now called Alitalia SAI (Società Aerea Italiana), was an ambitious one with a brand new management team headed by President Luca Cordero di Montezomolo, at the helms of Ferrari till a few months earlier,

Silvano Cassano as the new General Manager, Giancarlo Schisano as Chief Operations Officer and Etihad's Duncan Naysmith as Chief Financial Officer. General Manager of Etihad, James Hogan, pleased with the marriage between Alitalia and Etihad commented it was a particularly, 'good bargain' for Alitalia. What was in store for the newlyweds? By 2017 Alitalia was expected to generate €3.7 billion of business and return a profit of €108 million. Their aim was to increase revenues to almost €4.5 billion in 2023 bringing in a respectable profit of €212 million provided the industrial strategies adopted functioned without major hitches. How did they aim to do this? Without sacrificing short to mid-range routes, they aimed to focus on long haul flights which are more profitable from the Rome hub but also involve Milan's Malpensa in the act. The new routes were in the making for a number of destinations including, Beijing, Shanghai, Seoul, Mexico City, San Francisco and Santiago, Chile. Over the next four years four new routes would start operating from Rome, and Malpensa would more than double its long distance flights reaching 25 per week. Meanwhile the 134 planes Alitalia had would be increased by seven long-distance carriers to cope with the new slots acquired.

How would all this be achieved? By streamlining of costs already mentioned but also through massive investment. Etihad contributed €400 million to raise the new company's capital, and would acquire Alitalia Loyalty program for €112.5 million and spend €60 million to purchase slots at London Heathrow.

None of this helped. By 2017, Alitalia was again in deep trouble, losing some €490 million in 2016 and was desperately looking for new cash, again. The Government lent Alitalia €600 to keep the national airline operating and began looking for new buyers/partners. Lufthansa made a bid but asked for substantial reduction in employees, meanwhile, late Autumn 2017 UK's Easy Jet teaming up with US investment firm, Cerberus, made an offer, actually presented a plan and were willing to involve the government and trade unions to find a feasible, hopefully profitable, partnership for all concerned.

Talk of airlines and flights, low-cost or otherwise, brings to mind places we all desire to visit. The choice of destination naturally depends on our interests, one such interest can be visiting the most liveable place in a country where citizens enjoy the best quality of life, for your information the most liveable area in Italy for the year 2014 was the province of Ravenna and namesake capital. What's it like? Who and how do they decide where this 'paradise' is every year? It's all revealed in the next chapter.

TWENTY

RAVENNA, ITALY'S MOST LIVEABLE PROVINCE

Since 1990, every year Italy's leading financial daily, Il Sole 24 Ore, has published updated rankings of life conditions in Italy's 110 provinces; it is an interesting, widely reported and commented list informing on the quality of life up and down Italy. According to the paper's investigation, in 2014 the most liveable province enjoying the best quality of life was Ravenna in the Emilia-Romagna region of central Italy. How is this ranking compiled anyway? Numerous parameters subdivided into several sections including the environment, health services, employment, transport, social services, safety and crime rate, are considered, and points awarded for each; apparently in 2014 Ravenna scores were highest in the final classification.

In a little more detail, Ravenna came first in the supply of health and other social services and the quality of environment. Nurseries, in short supply in most places, are plentiful in Ravenna, more than double the national average where mothers can leave their young children to be looked after at a reasonable charge and hold on to a job as well. In Italy there's what's known as health migration whereby citizens travel to a different part of Italy seeking better quality healthcare, in the case of Ravenna only 3% of the local population opted for this against the national average of 9%. Processing civil court cases, painfully slow in Italy, was much faster here. Employment rate is also good, 67% of the population works. The ratio between the under 15 and over 64, stands at 121 to 87, the best in the country, looks like couples are not afraid of having children here probably because it's relatively easier to get a job and they get good services like affordable nurseries to help them raise a family.

Ravenna, the capital of the namesake province, with a manageable population of around 165,000 not only has favourable living and working conditions but enjoys a number of geographical as well as historical advantages. It is a seaside town about 53 km coastline drive to the north of the more famed resort town of Rimini and boasts nine beaches, or lidos, where the citizens can go, and attract tourism too. The municipality controls the largest territory in Italy second to only Rome in terms of acreage. Its history is a fascinating one and in some ways rivals that of the Eternal City.

Ravenna captured the slightest of interest of the Romans in 89 BC. At the time it was inhabited by a mixture of ancient populations, or their descendants, such as Etruscans and Umbrians as well as migrants from the East Mediterranean, who lived on small islands surrounded by marshy land much like Venice and engaged in fishing. In 31 BC Emperor Augustus realized Ravenna had a good position for a military harbour and he had one built here, calling it Classe, today the port area still carries this name, the city itself is some 8 km from the coast but is linked to the sea via Candiano Canal. In the year 402 AD Ravenna became the capital of Western Roman Empire taking over the privilege from Milan till the empire actually collapsed in 476 under attack from Ostrogoths. The same German tribe established the Kingdom of Ostrogoths in 493 ruled by King Theoderic the Great and maintained Ravenna as capital till 553. When Byzantine Justinian I became the new emperor controlling the Eastern Roman Empire in 527 he sent his best general Flavius Belisarius in 535 to conquer territory lost to Ostrogoths in Italy, Vandals in Africa and Visigoths in Spain. Ravenna was conquered in 540, it took 14 more years to conquer the rest of Italy. Ravenna eventually became a Byzantine protectorate serving as capital in Italian peninsula between 568 and 751 until taken over by the Lombards to be passed on to the church and control of the Pope in Rome even though keeping a degree of independence at times.

Pope Adrian I authorized Holy Roma Emperor Charlemagne to take what he wanted in Ravenna, excepting religious artefacts, the emperor obliged on three separate visits by removing all he can from Roman columns, statuary to Byzantine era mosaics to his capital, Aachen in Germany. Save an interlude in 13th century when Traversari family ruled, Ravenna remained a part of Papal States till the Da Polenta dynasty established the city-state there in 1275 and held on to it till the arrival of Venetians in 1440 who became the new rulers for the next seven decades or so. Around 1512 Ravenna returned to the Papal States again. In 1630 devastating floods initiated the building of a network of canals, swamps were drained and sizeable agricultural land developed over the next three centuries to the benefit of the Ravenna citizens. In 1861 Ravenna was incorporated into the newly born Kingdom of Italy that would eventually become the Republic of Italy in 1946.

This wealth of history left a wealth of monuments in the city; in 1996 UNESCO listed eight them of them as World Heritage Sites. All eight are religious buildings erected in 5th and 6th centuries and are beautiful, precious exemplars of early Christian architecture and decoration techniques mixing Romanesque and Byzantine styles. Spread around the city these sacred buildings, some of them housing museums, are what tourists come to see in Ravenna besides going to the beaches of course. Walking around the city, going inside the churches, chapels and museums you realise historical figures related to Ravenna are all still present in the awesome mosaics, or their remains are kept in mausoleums going back 1,500 years or more.
Ravenna's eight World Heritage Sites are:
1. Mausoleum of Galla Placidia
2. Basilica of San Vitale
3. Baptistery of Neon
4. Archiepiscopal Chapel
5. Arian Baptistery

6. Mausoleum of Theodoric
7. Basilica of Sant'Appolinare Nuovo
8. Basilica of Sant'Appolinare in Classe

The heart of the city is the spacious, pedestrianised, Piazza del Popolo, surrounded by historical buildings with two columns on the western side erected in 1483 by the Venetians. On top of the columns where St Mark's lion once stood symbolising Venetian power today stands a statue of St Vitalis, an early Christian martyr, on one and St Apollinaris, the first bishop of Ravenna, on the other, both are revered as patron saints in Ravenna. Behind the columns is Palazzo Comunale (municipal building) of late 17th century forming an L with Palazzo Veneziana which as the name implies was put up by the Venetians in 1461. As everywhere here too older buildings were used as quarries for new ones, the columns forming arches and porticoes were 'borrowed' from the 6th-century, St Andrews church constructed by the Goths, on three of the capitals can still be seen the monogram of Theodoric.

History aside the Piazza del Popolo is a lively square especially on a Saturday morning when farm produce is displayed everywhere and as in centuries past the townspeople gather for a bit of food shopping and gossip. On other days cafés with outdoor seating, people taking a coffee or lunch break bring the place alive, tourists wandering around, taking photos add more life still.

From outside the Mausoleum of Galla Placidia, situated to the north west of the city, doesn't appear impressive, a Palladian, Greek temple-like form with three blind arches is surmounted by a cube covered with a pyramidal roof. Two short extensions to each side complete the small building which was once a chapel in the Santa Croce church nearby. The interior on the other hand is truly impressive and exemplifies the magnificent mosaics decorating the inside of Ravenna's sacred buildings dating back to 5th century. The domed, deep blue ceiling with glittering stars, a golden cross in the middle is impressive, in the four corners we see a lion, an ox, an eagle and a man all of them winged symbolising the four evangelists, Mark, Luke, John and Matthew respectively. A lower semi-circular ceiling depicts red, white fruit interspersed by light blue flowers and golden leaves; on a semi-circular panel perpendicular to the ceiling facing the visitor entering is an image of a beardless Christ holding a golden cross herding sheep. In another ceiling scenery we see a lunette depicting St Peter carrying a key and St Paul both donning white togas appealing to Christ above them, between them, at their feet is a small fountain with two white doves symbolising lost souls in search of salvation. As this is a mausoleum there are also three sarcophagi one for Galla Palicidia, her husband General Constantinus III and son Valentinian III. The sarcophagi are of Roman origin meaning these marble tombs decorated with bass-reliefs are recycled material. One interesting question is, who is Galla Placidia anyway to deserve a mausoleum built just for her and family?

When the imperial court of Western Roman Empire was moved from Milan to Ravenna early 5th century, a church building frenzy took hold, the mausoleum, and Santa Croce next door, was where the imperial court probably decided to reside. It all began in 402 with Emperor Honorius, Galla Placidia's half brother, moving to Ravenna as Milan was deemed too hard to guard against attack, a seaside location surrounded by swamps was easier to defend. In 409 the Goths led by King Alaricus sack Rome but Ravenna is spared, born Aelia Galla Placidia in Ravenna in 392, the daughter of Theodosius the Great, emperor of the Eastern Roma Empire, is taken prisoner. In 413 Placidia marries Alaricus' son, Ataulf, in Narbonne, France. At Ataulf's death three years later, she is returned to her brother Honorius as a peace condition with Goths and is forced by Honorius into marriage with General Constantinus in 417. In 421 Constantinus is declared co-emperor with Honorius and Galla Placida an empress. Alas, Canstantinus dies seven months later, in Sep 421, at which point Valentinian III is declared emperor with Placida his tutor, Honorius almost blind at the time had no children to claim the title and passed away in

423. Over the next quarter of a century Ravenna would live a peaceful, prosperous period until her death in 450 probably in Rome not Ravenna, the sarcophagus that is supposed to contain her remains is in fact empty but there's a fairy tale like explanation for this. There is a deep hole on the back at the bottom of the sarcophagus, apparently in 16th century some curious individual inserted a lit candle through it to take a peek, the remains caught fire and burned.

Down the road from Mausoleum of Galla Placidia stands the Basilica of San Vitale whose construction began in 527 by the Goths and took 21 years to complete. It is an extraordinary example of Romanesque architecture using thin, 4-cm thick bricks, windows and cupola mixed with Byzantine style of building with polygonal apse, round bell tower and mosaics like in the Mausoleum of Galla Placidia but with a difference, there aren't only strictly religious scenes from the life of Christ, saints, prophets like Abraham and Moses, and Christian symbols; there are also copious bird, flower and vine depictions; we literally see history on the walls. There's a sizeable mosaic of Byzantine Emperor Justinian I and his court on one side and his wife Empress Theodora and her court on the other.

Walking down the artery Via G. Rasponi that leads off from Piazza del Popolo towards the city cathedral, Duomo, you get to see two other World Heritage Sites: Baptistery of Neon and Archiepiscopal Chapel close to one another. The cruciform chapel, situated on the second floor of Archiepiscopal Palace (Palazzo Arcivescovile), now a museum, was built to the orders of bishop Peter II in 495 and has wonderful mosaics depicting the four archangels Gabriel, Michael, Uriel and Raphael as well as the four evangelists. A lunette facing the entrance shows Christ as warrior holding a cross over this shoulder with a lion and snake at his feet clearly hinting at destroying the enemies of his creed which at the time included the so-called Arians who did not believe in trinity (the god, son and holy spirit) only in god as one. One reason the

UNESCO added it to their list explaining: "The significance of this property is the fact that it is the only Early Christian private oratory that has survived to the present day. Its iconography is also important by virtue of its strongly anti-Arian symbolism." Theodoric the Great was Arian and this chapel is the only one built during his reign that did not uphold Arian Christianity.

A short distance away stands the Neon Baptistery built some 50 years before the Archiepiscopal Chapel and decorated around 458 with the usual striking mosaics, it was finally completed at the end of 5th century by Bishop Neon. It's octagonal, like all baptisteries, symbolising the seven days of the week and eighth for resurrection and eternal life. The central mosaic decorating the cupola depicts St John standing in River Jordan baptising Jesus, around them the 12 apostles are shown in procession. There are eight lunettes acting as windows, over them are stucco decorations dating back to 5th century. On the floor a centrally located fountain, surrounded by arched niches create a harmonious ambiance. The UNESCO's reason for adding it to World Heritage Sites says it all: "This is the finest and most complete surviving example of the Early Christian baptistery, retains the fluidity in representation of the human figure derived from Greco-Roman art."

Both the Archiepiscopal Chapel and the Neon Baptistery were once part of the nearby cathedral that began life towards the end of 4th century when the episcopal seat was moved from Classe to Ravenna by Bishop Ursus. Alas, in 1734 it was demolished to make way for the new cathedral, modernisation apparently is not a recent phenomenon.

A 10-minute walk or so from Piazza del Popolo takes to another awesome World Heritage Site: Basilica of Sant'Appolinare Nuovo, built to the orders of Theodoric the Great during the first quarter of 6th century naturally respecting the doctrine of Arianism. Easily identified with its tall, round belfry, it was re-consecrated by Bishop Agnello as a Catholic place of worship in 561 and changed its name from Jesus Christ the Redeemer to St Martin in Heaven. In 856 the remains of Sant'Apollinare were transferred here from Basilica of Sant'Apollinare in Classe to escape danger from pirates and was renamed again and to distinguish it from its cousin by the harbour in Classe, Nuovo (new) was added, clear?

What's in Sant'Appolinare Nuovo? A simple setting of three naves with 12 Corinthian marble columns on each side, the same number as apostles and lots of mosaics. On the left 13 panels at the top close to the ceiling narrate the miracles and parables of Jesus Christ from the healing of a paralytic to the multiplication of bread and fish. Large panels just over the columns depict 22 virgins, and the three wise men taking gifts to child Jesus sitting on the lap of Madonna seated on a throne between four angels. On the right hand wall, at the top, 13 panels narrate biblical tales like the last supper, Judas kiss, Pontius Pilate washing his hands and resurrection of Christ. The larger lower panels shows 26 martyrs making their way towards Christ the Redeemer. On both walls are also images of prophets and saints, naturally. On one portion we see the harbour city of Classe stylized as a crenellated wall with tops of monuments hanging over it, next to it another panel shows us three boats symbolising the harbour, there's also a mosaic showing Theodoric's palace, the real one has long faded into history despite a ruin in the city is still wrongly called, Palazzo di Teodorico.

Of the other two UNESCO sites, Mausoleum of Theodoric, is about 1.5 km to the north-east of Ravenna and the other, Basilica of Sant'Apollinare in Classe, as the name implies is in Classe by the harbour. The Mausoleum of Theodoric was built to the order of the king as his future tomb in 520 and is the only monument in Ravenna of that period that is not a brick building but stone blocks imported for Istria. Built as two tiers a ten-sided lower tier and an upper part, one single block weighing 300 tons with a smaller diameter of 10 metres. Inside a porphyry sarcophagus without a lid once indeed contained Theodoric's bones, when Justinian conquered the city, the remains were swiftly disposed of. It made the list of UNESCO because of its singular Gothic style and that it is the only surviving tomb of a king from that era. Interestingly it is set in an ancient necropolis hence the location of the tomb is far from coincidental.

A short drive following the signposts for Rimini leads to the Basilica of Sant'Apollinare in Classe standing in open countryside 5 km away with its round bell tower on the side erected in 10th century, a replica of the one put up for Sant'Apollinare Nuovo. Considered the largest basilica of early Christendom, it was built to the orders of Bishop Ursicinus but paid for by a Greek banker called Iulianus Argentarius, the same wealthy individual also totally funded the construction of the Basilica of San Vitale. It was finally consecrated by Bishop Maximianus in 549. In 1756 excavation work in the area discovered a Christian cemetery here but also numerous pagan tomb stones, looks like material from an ancient necropolis was recycled to pave the basilica. Interior with one nave and two aisles separated by 24 veined marble columns is again lavishly decorated. The apse dome shows Christ standing under a large cross on each side of him are the profiles of six sheep in procession, as backdrop we see greenery most likely the pine wood Ravenna is till famous for. There are other 6th century mosaics, above the large cross again we see six lambs in procession on each side and above them, below the ceiling, a medallion of a bearded Christ is flanked by the four evangelists disguised as winged lion, calf, eagle and man. Between the four windows behind the altar, are the mosaics of four bishops responsible for the building of Ravenna's basilicas: Ursicinus, Ursus, Severus and Ecclesius. The frescoes above the columns on the other hand depict Ravenna's archbishops but are of 18th century material. There are other fascinating details, as for the mosaics and frescoes in other churches and basilicas in Ravenna but would require much more space to go into here.

The importance of mosaics in Ravenna's churches cannot be emphasised enough. In these Byzantine-style mosaics often portray a beardless, youthful Jesus, no crucifixions or suffering are in sight. How to depict religious figures in art was a controversial issue at the time. In 692 the Council of Quinisext held in Constantinople passed 102 canons including official guidelines on how Jesus, the Virgin Mary and the saints should be painted. Only icons were to be allowed, human-like forms were outlawed. The Catholic Church in the West disagreed insisting on a more realistic figure underlining the human aspect of Jesus, the redeemer. This led to what's known as the iconoclastic war, in 726 Emperor Leo III based in Constantinople ordered the destruction of all images of Christ, Madonna and saints, any disobedience was severely punished despite the opposition by Pope Gregory II. Only at the margins of the empire, in places like Ravenna, original sacred artwork predating 726 survived. The tradition of portraying Jesus returned in 843 under the reign of Empress Theodora.

Another important monument in Ravenna is the tomb of Tuscan poet/politician Dante Alighieri (1265-1321), not a World Heritage Site but a major tourist attraction nevertheless. Why is Italy's most famous poet buried in Ravenna and not in Florence where he was born? It's all for his political views, or choices; in 1289 the political groups, Guelphs of Florence, and Ghibellines of Arezzo actually fought the Battle of Campaldino where Dante took part, Guelphs were victorious, alas, soon after the Guelphs divided into two factions as Whites, supporting the Pope, and Blacks aiming for limitation of papal power in Florentine affairs. Dante espoused the cause of the Whites, ensuing conflict and eventual supremacy of the Blacks aided by Charles of Valois, the brother of France's King Philip IV, led to the expulsion of families supporting the Whites in 1302, Dante had no choice but leave never to return. He lived in other cities including Rome, Verona,

Sarzana in Liguria and finally Ravenna as guest of Guido Novello Da Polenta for the last five years of his life and completed his masterpiece, Divina Commedia. A respectable tomb to honour him was only crafted in 1483 and the building that houses it came to be only in 1780. Ironically there's a handsome statue of Dante by the main entrance to Santa Croce Basilica in Florence, defined the repository of Italy's illustrious men with the tombs of the likes of Michelangelo, Galileo Galilei and Gioachino Rossini, and one bearing the epitaph: Dante Alighieri, Onorate l'altissimo poeta, meaning, Honour the most exalted poet; placed there in 1829 it's been empty ever since. Not that the Florentines didn't do anything to get the poets bones. When the Medici, ruling family in Florence, actually had two Medici kin elected popes, as Leo X in 1513 and again as Clement VII in 1730, they used all their power to bring the remains of the famous Florentine poet back home but to no avail. The Franciscan friars living in a monastery annexed to still standing St Francis church drilled a hole from an adjacent wall and removed the poet's bones, they lay hidden in a nearby oratory till 1865, on Dante's 600th anniversary of birth.

Twenty-first century Ravenna is busy keeping alive its huge historical, cultural heritage. Over the last 16 centuries since the earliest Christian buildings went up, numerous churches not mentioned above still stand just as many have disappeared. The area between Ravenna and Classe contains a wealth of archaeological treasures waiting or being excavated. The Classe area itself has been transformed into a an archaeological park starting 2000 and was open to visitors, alas in 2012 an unexploded bomb dating from WWII was discovered, yes, a historical city like Ravenna was bombed during both WWI and II but all damage has long been repaired. The area was closed off to the public while the entire park was being made safe to visit, finally all safety problems were solved and the park-museum inaugurated in July 2015.

Ever since Roman times Ravenna and its surrounds has had pine woods and wetlands. Currently 2,000 hectares divided up into several separate woods extend to the north and south of the Candiano Canal; in 18th century it was three and a half times more extensive and was just one big continuous pine forest. Wetlands known as Punte Alberete and Valle della Canna, around 10 km to the north going in the direction of Venice, are protected, natural reserve areas covering some 450 hectares and are home to healthy wildlife, acting as oases of peace and quiet no doubt helping Ravenna to be voted the most liveable place in Italy. Since 2014, Ravenna has lost its place at the top, ranking 10th, 12th and slipping to 23rd place in 2015, 2016 and 2017 respectively but that doesn't stop it offering all the above attractions.

What about the capital, Rome, you may be interested to learn that it was placed 24th in 2017, just below Ravenna, but remains one of Italy's most popular destinations, as is Lazio, the region it is situated in.

TWENTY-ONE

TRIP TO LAZIO

Our neighbour Michela, a retired care worker in her sixties, recently got the travel bug. She is always on the lookout for seaside holidays, weekend breaks or day trips on a shoestring budget. When I asked her where she was going next, she showed me the itinerary for a 6-day trip to Lazio, the Italian region served by Rome as capital, late April 2017. It was a bus tour taking in a number of places I wanted to visit, I looked at the price tag and couldn't believe it, including all the meals it came to just €450. I asked if they still had room for two, me and my wife. The next day, she confirmed they did, we signed on. It would turn out one of the most quirky, 'eventful' trips I've ever taken.

When the departure day came upon us, we took the bus from where we live at 5:25 am, it was till dark, and slowly headed for the pick-up point in the outskirts of Como, our home by the namesake lake in Northern Italy. The appointment was at 6:00 a.m. and Signor Luigi, the tour organiser, had strongly recommended we arrive at the bus stop possibly a little earlier than 6:00. We even had our seat numbers, just like on a plane, amazing organisation I kept thinking, then again Luigi was a retired policeman hence discipline and orderly conduct, strictly following the itinerary, and timetable, was only to be expected. We had been told to keep the same seats for the whole of the trip to avoid disorder that may easily degenerate into chaos, and possible arguments, every time we got off and on the bus. Seemed like Luigi had thought of everything. We got to the agreed pick-up point at exactly 5:50, feeling awfully organised, there was already half a dozen people there waiting in the chilly, early hours of the day rubbernecking, expecting the bus to turn up at any moment. Well, it pulled in at

6:20, and we started feeling a little disappointed, perhaps they encountered unexpected traffic, but seemed unlikely at that time of morning, I personally began having some doubts about Luigi's organisation skills even if these doubts were not really justifiable at this stage, they may have had to wait for someone. Actually, his wife was assisting him, while her husband supervised the loading of our bags, she ushered us onto the bus waving her hand from side to side ordering us, albeit with a broad smile on her face, to hurry as if it wasn't the bus but we who arrived late.

  The bus was virtually full with only two seats free at the very back, we were in the second but last row and risked motion sickness if the journey took too long and there were too many bends to negotiate. When I mentioned it to Luigi, he showed his human face reassuring us that he would willingly give up his seat next to the driver for us to take a break, in turn, if necessary.

  Off we went towards the city of Orvieto, the first leg of our trip, some 500 km away. I'd been to this interesting city in the region of Umbria that neighbours with Lazio and Tuscany about 20 years before and wondered how it changed if at all. Driving through damp weather with thick clouds hanging above us we stopped at a petrol station with restaurant service for lunch, the only meal we had to pay extra. It soon became clear Luigi, besides his wife, had at least two other assistants, Angelo, likeable, polite, who came round every now and again asking us if everything was alright, if we needed water (they had some bottled for sale), the other, a retired police officer everyone called General, was of Roman origins and sounded like a history teacher, especially versed in Roman history. Luigi using the bus microphone kept going over and over the itinerary giving out detailed, very detailed, information about what we were going to see and couldn't stress enough how expensive the local guides were and that we should take full advantage of their services and not disappear the minute we arrived in Orvieto for instance. We began socialising with Michela's friends, two nurses, and a retired carpenter who loved ballroom dancing, he kept reminding Michela, also a keen dancer, that Luigi promised there would be music and dancing in the hotel every night and that he couldn't wait to get on the dance floor to show off his skills doing the Tango, Waltz, Fox Trot, even Boogie-Woogie. During the drive it seemed most of the people knew each other, and chatted away cracking endless jokes, especially Luigi and the General, most of them too dirty to repeat here needless to say. Occupying the very back seats was a quiet, Italian-speaking couple from Switzerland, he a freelance physiotherapist who gave up a well-paid job in a bank to escape stressful corporate life and enjoy some freedom, so he said, she an unemployed teacher with a permanent falsetto voice doing voluntary work teaching children with learning disabilities. They swore by alternative medicine, enjoyed yoga and meditation; their motto seemed to be: Peace on Earth, Live and Let Live. The physiotherapist at some point revealed he possessed what he called psychic magnetism, seeing my puzzled expression he explained. "By the power of my mind I can make things happen," seeing me getting even more puzzled, he gave an example, "I was in Paris last year and not having booked a place to stay I was driving around looking for affordable accommodation when I suddenly remembered a close friend who'd moved to Paris many years ago; we'd exchanged some messages over the years and every time he would invite me to stay with him and his family if I ever came to Paris, I stopped the car and called him, he was truly pleased to hear from me and said yes of course he would love me to spend a few days with them. He gave me the address, guess what? I'd parked right in front of his house! I tried my best to look stunned but all the time I kept thinking, 'coincidence.' He seemed so convinced he had psychic powers I decided not to challenge him and spoil the magic revelation.

  Shortly before our arrival in Orvieto Luigi came up to me and asked if I minded carrying the blue flag representing our group, he recommended I stay close to the guide as the trip would be filmed, why me I couldn't help enquiring, he bent down and whispered in my ear, "Besides being a professional journalist, you're also the youngest, and best looking..."); embarrassed, I couldn't but accept this enormous responsibility, with one arm nearly always up in the air, how am I going to take photos, I thought.

Compared to my first arrival in Orvieto on a sunny August afternoon with the light hurting my eyes, this time I was met with rain and a chilly wind, I had already put away my sunglasses. Our local guide was all smiles hiding under an umbrella, and I encountered yet another problem, with one arm already occupied, I needed another arm to hold an umbrella, meaning it was impossible to take a photo, luckily my wife came to my aid offering me protection under her umbrella. The guide, very friendly and upbeat despite the imperfect weather conditions, walked around the city centre with us, indicating all the interesting sights. The main attraction of the ancient city is the truly magnificent, gothic cathedral decorated with golden mosaics narrating, as expected, biblical stories. She did however, point out some details I really didn't think much about the last time I was here. On the facade, at eye level, there are four panels of bas-reliefs. The first two illustrate stories from the Old Testament, the third from New Testament documenting episodes from the life of Jesus, and the last, well, is on the Last Judgment, or Doomsday if you prefer. But why the necessity for such striking narration, as if telling a tale with real, three-dimensional people? It was, apparently, to really impress the ordinary folk into submission to the will of God, as illiteracy was high, what better way to convey the message of God than with impressive, 3-D images.

The other details I couldn't recall included the several souvenir shops displaying beautifully crafted pottery and an old building, Torre di Maurizio, to the left of the cathedral, which I hadn't take much notice of. The guide pointed out the automaton on the roof, "It was placed there in 1349 and struck the time every 15 minutes," she said, "reminding the workers busy constructing the cathedral of the passage of time, perhaps reminding them to hurry or hopefully that it was time take a lunch break." This mechanical contraption hitting on a bell with a hammer is the oldest of its kind in Italy, after that of Venice's. I didn't know that.

Wandering around the city's car-free, cobblestone streets, passing by medieval monuments, a tall tower called, Torre Civica, churches and more, with intermittent drizzle impeding our enjoyment, we came to one sight that I did remember, Pozzo di San Patrizio, or St Patrick's Well, although again the details escaped me except that it is a really deep well. The guide, God bless her, refreshed my memory. It all began in 1528, the year after Rome was sacked by the mercenaries obeying to Charles V, the Holy Roman Emperor, the then Pope Clement VII escaped to the hilltop, walled town of Orvieto taking up residence in a palace there. What to do about water supply in case of a long siege? He ordered the building of an extraordinary well that ran some 60 metres deep and took some nine years to realise. Cylindrical in shape, 13 metres in diameter with a double helix staircase ensured water could be transported to the top without the transporters, and their animals, on the way up never crossed paths with traffic going down the shaft. Lighting? Forget impractical candles or torches, 72 windows were built to make sure there was enough visibility despite descending to the bowels of the Earth. Why name it after St Patrick's, Ireland's patron saint? Legend would have us believe that there is a cave in Ireland on Station Island in Donegan County known as Patrick's Purgatory, it was indicated to the saint by Jesus as the entrance to purgatory proper. The site appeared on maps in 15th century, hence, bearing in mind the depth of the well in Orvieto, Clement VII thought it was an apt name. In case you're wondering how I managed to take photos in Orvieto, again my beloved wife came to my aid and became the standard-bearer giving me a few moments to frame and shoot.

At 5:30 pm, more or less, we left rainy Orvieto and drove to our hotel, Belvedere Mentana, in the namesake township, 107 km away, looking forward to our welcome dinner. The hotel seemed very busy, a sizeable Chinese group occupied one dining area, a Polish group another, another still was for Koreans, a long table was reserved for Luigi and his regulars, six-seven of us, including Michela and her nurse friends, sat at a round table. We soon befriended the couple in their sixties sitting with us, after a short while it seemed they had five grown-up children, they kept mentioning them, two daughters were vegan, so hard to travel with them looking for the right food, I asked how long they'd been married, they briefly looked at each other and confessed they were just living together, and the 'kids' were from former marriages. I decided not to ask any more personal questions. The dinner was nothing to write home about, it was a fixed menu, we couldn't choose anything, an unexciting pasta dish was followed by bland pork escalopes, and a dessert of the hotel's choice...the only flavour you could taste was...sweet, I left it unfinished. Wine? Yes, red house wine, unremarkable as all house wines usually are. Michela and her friends not to mention the retired carpenter were looking forward to some dancing after dinner, probably to forget about the insipid dinner experience. Luigi came over to ask how everything was, none of us showed much enthusiasm, Michela enquired about the whereabouts of the dancing hall, Luigi assumed a pained expression, "We couldn't get permission to play copyrighted music in public, they said we had to pay, much too expensive, sorry." Yes, in Italy playing copyrighted recorded music in public requires permission and payment of a fee from SIAE (Società Italiana degli Autori ed Editori).

    After coffee, an extra we had to pay for out of our own pockets, we decided to go to bed, still, tomorrow we were going to Tivoli, only 20 km away, to visit two fantastic villas, Villa di Adriana and Villa d'Este, really looked forward to that. On the way to our room I stopped at the reception and asked the wifi password, the receptionist informed me that it wasn't free, cost €4 an hour, or €10 for the whole day. For the first time ever I was being asked to pay to use wifi in a hotel. I said I'd think about it and headed to our room, comfortable, spacious I'd say, even had a tiny TV set, a cathode tube version with no remote mind you, still, we could at least watch the news.

Next morning we rushed to have breakfast, an exciting day was awaiting us, the breakfast consisted of cappuccino, brioche (nobody says croissant in Italy) orange juice (not the freshly squeezed type), bread, butter and jam, even honey, no sign of cereal, yogurt, cheese, fresh fruit, eggs or any other ingredient normally served, when I enquired, the waiter said I could buy them at the bar, as I don't eat croissant, I went and bought some fruit and low fat yogurt for a few euros, something I would repeat for the rest of our stay there. It was now becoming crystal clear, a budget holiday is exactly that, and as the saying goes, you get what you pay for. As I walked past the Koreans' dining area, I envied them their long table laid with a rich array of breakfast items they could just help themselves to. For a minute I considered joining them, pretending I was one of the group but I'd be spotted immediately, I hardly look Korean.

At 9:30, the specified time Luigi kept reminding us the day before, threatening to leave behind anyone who was late, we were in our seats way at the back, we waited a good 15 minutes for two of Luigi's entourage, they had to have a second coffee and there was a long queue at the bar. Luigi warned them to be punctual next time. Despite being the last days of April, it was another cloudy, drizzly day (despite complaints by most of us for substandard dinner and breakfast, we didn't blame this on Luigi). I had our flag in my rucksack ready to take out on our arrival in Tivoli. The moment we hit the road, we had to grind to a halt, well, a crawl, there were tailbacks everywhere, many of the townspeople were commuting to work in Rome and the traffic was truly heavy. Luigi trying to distract us began informing us of what we would see that day, again, there would be a local guide to explain what we were looking at, by the way, he said, today we'll have a packed lunch, enjoy the day.

Some 45 minutes later, we reached Villa Adriana and met our guide, a tall woman in her forties with a high pitched voice, she really had to shout to make herself heard by everyone, as I had to stay close to her holding our flag in the air, she was basically screaming into my ear. I soon found a way to put distance between me and her, she too had a flag of her own, like all guides who lead the way like the piper player in Rat-Catcher of Hamelin with the rats trailing behind him, hence there was no need for both us to hold one up, Luigi seemed puzzled at first but then yielded and I was free to take photos using both hands. As she led us up to the villa, I noticed a town sprawling on a hilltop in the distance, and asked the guide if she minded identifying, it, "That's Tivoli," she responded, then where are we now I couldn't help enquiring, "in the outskirts of Tivoli," she echoed nonchalantly

I was expecting to see an Italian villa, a nice old, perhaps multi-storey building with landscaped gardens and ponds, instead judging by the model of the site displayed in a small pavilion, this was more like a small village covering some 120 hectares and would take 3-4 hours to visit. It was realised starting 118 AD to the orders of Roman emperor, Hadrian, and took over a dozen years to complete. After 1,900 years or so, of the 30 or so buildings, pools, farmland and gardens the site originally comprised, only ruins have remained but they still tell a fascinating story.

A well-travelled man, Hadrian imported various building styles from Rome Empire's provinces, especially Greece and Egypt. He apparently wanted to remember the places and monuments he saw and admired during his sojourns in the Orient like the Academy, Pecile (large pool surrounded by columns and gardens) in Athens, and Canopus Channel situated in the Nile delta. After an introduction by the guide shouting at us huddled around the site model, with frequent interjections from the General filling in details the guide supposedly have left behind, we began our tour of the famed archaeological complex in earnest, we walked past a tall brick wall that once surrounded the site, it began to drizzle, protected under our umbrellas we took a glimpse of the Pecile right before us, the pool was there all right but the columns had disappeared and was surrounded by a stretch of overgrown grass rather than a garden with pretty flowers, in Hadrian's time it was probably much more colourful and attractive.

Trailing our guide we took in an amazing array of archaeological gems, no wonder Hadrian's Villa is a World Heritage Site since 1999 and is still being excavated, in 2013 a network of tunnels was discovered under the villa grounds thought to have been used by the servants commuting from one place to another. Go past the Pecile we came to the Imperial Palace, Library, Baths, and reached, Canopus, perhaps the most striking creation at the site with a pool 121 metres long 18 metres wide surrounded by partly standing Corinthian columns and statues reflecting on the green water. It is believed Hadrian and his guests had picnics and parties here. Beyond Canopus was the Academy, situated at the highest point of the site, and overlooking the Canopus the spacious Praetorius Esplanade and ruins of adjacent buildings believed to have been warehouses led us to the Greek Library and another small but impressive structure, the Maritime Theatre, despite its name this is a small villa with a circular channel and columns surrounding it; one of the first buildings to be erected on the site, it was probably where Hadrian lived while the Imperial Palace was being constructed.

Equally pleased with our visit to Villa Adriana and that the rain had abated, we were back on the bus having a rest after all the walking and standing about listening to the guide; our next destination was Tivoli itself beckoning us from the hilltop. A short drive later we were discharged at the busy town centre, it was lunchtime by then and we took our packed lunches out of our bags and rucksacks wondering what they actually contained. Nothing exciting, a couple of cheese and ham rolls, a bottle of still water and a banana. We made our way to Villa d'Este nearby, another UNESCO World Heritage Site, right next to Santa Maria Maggiore church. This was where we would spend a few hours before heading back to the hotel in Mentana. We were in for a surprise.

I had heard of this villa famed for its fountains but wasn't really prepared for the spectacular exemplars I'd find there. Designed by Pirro Ligorio, built in 16th century also employing materials and statuary scavenged from Villa Adriana, it was what I'd expected an Italian villa to be after all I've visited many of them along the shores of Lake Como where I live, actually we too have a Villa d'Este near Como dating to 16th century which is now a luxury hotel but is no match for the size of landscaped gardens and numerous fountains we would see in Tivoli.

A courtyard, originally cloisters, embellished with statues and flowers and the Fountain of Venus lead into the villa proper. Beautifully frescoed rooms one after the after was where Ippolito II d'Este, the cardinal who commissioned the building of the villa, resided in great comfort and luxury. Walking onto a balcony we looked down at the terraced gardens opening up before us and the countryside beyond. As there were a good number of retired people among us well into their seventies, the guide warned, "Remember there's no lift to bring you back up, so the further down you go the further really uphill distance you'll have to climb." Staircase after staircase, walking trail after walking trail most of us easily descended to the bottom and saw the facade of the villa meant to be observed from the gardens, in the past visitors entered the grounds from the bottom and had to walk up and admire the gardens, statues and villa above them.

There are indeed a bewildering number of fountains, one walkway is named, The Hundred Fountains, there aren't that many lining the walkway but dozens of masks one after the other squirt water towards you as you walk past. The most spectacular ones must be Fountain of the Neptune and Fountain of the Organ below it where a cascade of water flows into a series of pools from where several jets of water explode into the air. The scenery is completed with three rectangular fish ponds further on. Other eye-catching fountains include the Fountain of the Rometta, or little Rome, that includes an obelisk rising from a boat symbolising the Tiburtina Island where Rome was founded, and Fountain of Ovata (oval) with a statue of the Greek oracle, Sybil Albunesa, surmounting the ensemble. Listing all the fountains, literally hundreds, would take a long time but is worth mentioning the Fountain of Glass by Bernini, and the fountains of The Dragon, The Owl and Birds, and Diana of Ephesus.

After the thoroughly satisfying day at Tivoli, we were soon back at the hotel getting ready for dinner, we didn't expect anything remotely as satisfying but it seemed less important now. We were served a similar menu to the evening before, the pork escalopes again but with a different sauce, a few of us asked if we could have vegetable soup instead, waiter panicked for a minute, went away to enquire and came back beaming, yes, of course...for dessert we had fruit salad and all felt we at least had a healthy dinner even if it was far from gourmet experience. The carpenter, Michela and few other dancing enthusiasts discussed going into town and looking for a disco, a ballroom hall of sorts to dance the night away... meanwhile the rest of retired to our rooms fairly early, the following morning we had to leave the hotel at 7 and head for the island of Ponza for the day, we all looked forward to it and hoped the crossing wouldn't be rough.

It took more than two hours to reach the seaside town of San Circeo Felice to board the boat that would take us to Ponza about an hour's sail away, it was a sunny day, the sea seemed calm, it was bound to be a smooth crossing, and my wife Nadia was convinced she wouldn't need to chew any stomach calming gums she'd brought along.

Most of us sat in the lower, protected deck looking out of the window, some went onto the open, top deck to soak up some sunshine, it was the first day we'd had sunshine since the trip began. As we leaped forward full throttle, it felt like being in a motorboat 15-20 metres long. What seemed like fun at first, soon became bothersome, the sea wasn't as calm as it appeared, the sailors assisting us recommended we sat down and not go up and down the top deck. After 15 minutes Nadia and I began chewing our gums, and gave a few to the others sitting with us, Nadia keeping a couple for the return journey basically gave away all the gums she had brought along, she could have sold each one at a handsome price the demand was so high, everyone was asking her for one. A number of people were lying on the floor hoping this would stop them from being sick. An hour later, not exactly feeling 100%, we approached Ponza, very popular with Romans where many Italian celebrities own holiday homes.

    Mostly white and pastel coloured, low-rise houses framed a crescent -shaped harbour on the main island crowded with fishing boats, there are three other smaller islands, Palmarola, Gavi and Zannone nearby but we wouldn't have time to visit those, just as well, none of us had the 'stomach' for other crossings for the day and all dreaded the crossing back to the mainland late in the afternoon. Once off the boat, we all felt great all of a sudden and couldn't wait to explore the island, there was a local guide of course, a soft spoken lady in her sixties we all strained to hear, 10 minutes later only a dozen people still stuck around listening to her, the rest of us branched out to walk about the island as we pleased, it didn't take long to stroll down the main thoroughfare on the seafront lined mainly with picturesque restaurants, cafés and souvenir shops. Soon lunchtime was upon us, yes, we had packed lunches prepared by the hotel again, we sat at the small, sandy beach and munched away, awaiting 2:30 p.m. when a bus would take us on a tour of the rest of the island.

    The bus tour was rewarding indeed, as we needed two buses, the guide accompanied one group going and the other returning. The bus climbed and climbed and finally stopped at the highest point of the island where we could take a bird's eye view of the port and its surrounds, the pretty scenery unfolding below us deserved many camera clicks. On the other side we could see the ghostly outlines of the island of Ventotene. Descending we saw two bays, Cala Teola and Cala Dell'Acqua with picturesque ports. Our guide was the driver whose local accent I had trouble to decipher at first but soon managed to understand most of what he was saying, he pointed out the homes of many Italian notables, politicians, journalists, actors, singers and mentioned a number of international celebrities that visited the island in recent years including, Beyoncé, Rihanna, Bruce Springsteen and Michael Douglas. Ironically Ponza spent most of its existence as a prison starting the ancient Greeks who used it as a penal colony, during the 1920s Benito Mussolini sent his political opponents and dissidents to Ponza where he himself would be jailed for 10 days starting 27 July 1943.

During the return journey we briefly stopped at an arresting sandy beach, Chiaia di Luna, at the foot of white cliffs. All of a sudden we met a just-married couple still in their wedding attire enjoying a ride in a convertible Rolls Royce, all cameras swung from the beach to the vintage car. It was still a beautiful sunny day, we made our way to the boat awaiting us but nobody was keen to board. As we sailed again at full throttle, we were expecting to feel sick at any moment, no such thing happened, I went upstairs to the top deck to 'sunbathe', half way, some 30 minutes later, I could see the waves getting taller, the sea heaving a little more, all of a sudden rather than sunshine I was soaked with salty water, and rushed along with everybody else to the protected deck below. Nadia and I began chewing our medication against sea sickness. Looking around I noticed a lot of pale faces, an obese, elderly lady lost her balance and fell on the floor, it took two staff members spending most of their time handing out bags to sick or about to be sick passengers and three of us to get her on her feet and drag her to a seat. When she pulled herself together, she asked my wife, 'Is your husband going to write about us on this trip, he'll have a lot of interesting material." Nadia reassured her the writer would be discreet and not mock anyone, he might not even write anything about the trip, he's busy working on other projects. Little did they know. Arrival at San Circeo Felice was met with understandable relief, the two-hour bus journey to the hotel seemed a piece of cake, smooth sailing so to speak.

Dinner again consisted of a pasta, a meat dish followed by dessert, encouraged by the previous evening when some flexibility came our way, we asked if we could have something fishy or vegetarian instead pointing out my wife and I were pesco-vegetarians (actually we don't follow this diet religiously, if it's too much trouble, we adapt and eat meat too), to our surprise the waiter informed the chef and served us veggie burgers, fine by us, some of our party asked for ham and cheese but were flatly refused, it seemed they didn't mind serving you something cheaper than what was on the fixed menu but not anything more expensive. The following evenings we kept eating veggie burgers but that was OK, better than pork any day.

Next morning we were all excited to go to Rome to see the wonderful sights, we had all been there before but it was nice to see it in a different season. It was another beautiful sunny day, a balmy spring day, I wondered what had changed in the Eternal City since I last went there five years before. The Spanish Steps and the Trevi Fountain had been restored to their prior glory and I couldn't wait to see them gleaming in the sunshine. Checking the itinerary I realised it would be hard to see them unless I abandoned the group and went exploring by myself, I decided to wait and see.

All the way to central Rome, the General refreshed our memories of Roman Empire's history with amazing competence, he could remember so many names and dates I wondered if he'd 'revised' Roman history just to impress us during the trip. Apparently not, being born in Rome he grew up there surrounded by monuments breathing history and was truly familiar with the city. We asked Luigi why he bothered to pay a handsome fee to a guide when we had the General. The bus came to a halt not far from the church of Santa Maria in Cosmedin where the famous Bocca della Verità (mouth of truth) is placed, hordes of tourists have always gone there to have their photos taken by the disc bearing the semblance of a human face with open eyes, nostrils and mouth which began life as a drain cover in Roman times. People stick their hand into the gaping mouth and if they've been telling lies the mouth bites their hand. Visiting the church or taking selfies by Bocca della Verità was not scheduled, nor taking a look at the 300-year-old Two Tritons Fountain across the road from the church in a quiet square embellished by two still-standing Roman temples.

    The guide, a dark-haired woman in her thirties with a confident voice led the way to the nearby Teatro di Marcello (Theatre of Marcellus) which seemed like a miniature of Colosseum, the guide in fact pointed out many tourists mistake it for the Colosseum, I was surprised to hear the top tier of the ancient theatre has been transformed into apartments, very expensive ones I imagine. She then led us to the nearby Jewish Ghetto, as the name implies this is where the Jewish community was confined starting 1555, some 40 years after that of Venice, ordered by Pope Paul VI and would continue till 1848 when Pope Pious IX put an end to the confinement.

    We then took a walk to Piazza Venezia with bustling traffic crowding the large boulevards intersecting here, and tourists crowding the pavements, by that time we'd lost the guide; we climbed the stairway to Campidoglio (Capitol Hill) and stood amid a huge crowd with the bronze equestrian statue of Roman Emperor Marco Aurelio gazing at us sitting on his horse, from the handsome piazza designed by Michelangelo, we could see the ruins of the Forum below us. Many selfie takers permitting I managed to get a couple of shots with my camera and we fled the throngs only to meet more crowds by the Vittoriano, the huge monument inaugurated in 1911, on the 50th anniversary of Italy as a united country, erected to honour Italy's fallen war heroes. Speaking in many tongues many were again busy taking selfies. From Piazza Venezia a famed artery, Via dei Fori Imperiali, leads to Rome's most famous sight, the Colosseum. The artery created in 1932 to the orders of Mussolini to showcase his power at the expense of important Roman buildings, was finally pedestrianised in August 2013. We took a walk up this wide boulevard in the company of our guide until the Colosseum which was restored in recent years, with all the grime removed the underlying marble did seem to shine on this sunny day. Trailing our guide closely, after all she was taking us to a very interesting place, Ristorante Naumachia, for lunch. We were ushered to the spacious basement and began our best meal so far on this trip. The menu included cold cuts, the pasta dishes cacio e pepe and rigatoni all'amatriciana, Roman style veal dish, salti in bocca, roast potatoes, panna cotta for dessert and good red wine.

The lunch lasted well over two hours and there really wasn't much time left to see other famous sights like the Spanish Steps, Trevi Fountain or Piazza Navona, in fact our itinerary said we would take a walk in Trastevere, one of Rome's most atmospheric neighbourhoods literally 'across the Tevere,' or River Tiber, away from the city's famed sights mentioned before. Judging by the square leading to this ancient neighbourhood crowded with young people sitting on cobblestones listening to a live rock concert, it is just as popular with tourists. We trailed our guide to another piazza with a fountain in the middle with loads of tourists sunbathing on its steps and the 12th-century Basilica di Santa Maria beyond it drawing the attention. As the first sacred building in Rome dedicated to Virgin Mary, it bears a number of mosaics depicting Mary on the facade and inside. We trailed the guide into the basilica to take a look.

It's quite full, despite the brilliant sunshine outdoors, many are wandering around the semi-dark basilica scanning the religious artwork. Our guide breaks into a detailed description of the golden mosaics, realised between 12th and 13th century, covering the entire apse, they are believed to narrate the medieval procession held on the night of Assumption, all very interesting but then she starts talking about techniques of mosaic making and began to lose our attention, half a dozen of us drifted off to wander on our own and soon we were out in the sun strolling along narrow streets exploring picturesque Trastevere. At the agreed time we headed for the bus looking forward to being driven to Gianicolo, the hilltop location that gives a sweeping view of Rome below. Unfortunately, Luigi informed us that we didn't have time and that we would take a bus ride through Rome instead that didn't include Gianicolo, why put it on the itinerary then, many complained. The Swiss couple suddenly became vociferous, lamenting the lack of organisation and waste of time for the long lunch break. The bus ploughing through heavy traffic went by some famous sites like the Ara Pacis, an altar dedicated to Emperor Augustus, now restored and protected by glass casing, and Quirinale the palace where the Italian president resides. By 6:30 p.m. we were back at the hotel not particularly looking forward to dinner though we did look forward to visiting a monastery and the towns of Frascati and Ariccia set in Lazio's hilly countryside the following day. Before the end of dinner, I see Luigi abruptly getting up from his chair and storming to the reception area wearing a dark face. I went up to him to enquire, he admitted to having a furious argument with Angelo, "He interferes with everything," he complained, "I don't mind him helping out but he keeps criticising everything, I can't stand it any longer, and I told him so." I advised him not to take it too seriously, it's impossible to please everyone. He nodded, I could see he was already sorry for quarrelling with his friend. Before the night was out, I saw them talking in hushed tones, eventually Luigi put his arm around Angelo's shoulder, they briefly smiled at each other, I was pleased to see them make up.

    Early the next morning, we set off, drove through pleasant countryside, with lots crimson poppy flowers embellishing the fields even the roadside at times. Our first stop is at a curious monastery 32 km away that goes by the name of San Nilo in the small town of Grottaferrara, I'd never heard of either. It's a quiet place with hardly anyone around, then it struck me, it's May 1st, a national holiday. After a brief walk through a leafy park we head for the monastery, and meet our guide, a monk donning a heavy dark robe. He is surprisingly upbeat and friendly, seems more like a TV presenter talking entertainingly to an audience than a solemn cleric. He's obviously been entertaining and informing tourists for some time. The monastery, we learn, was founded by abbot Nilus of Rossano, a monk from Calabria of Greek descent, in 1004, half a century before the schism between the eastern and western Christianity that created Catholic and Greek Orthodox churches, and despite defining itself Catholic has always used Greek Orthodox rites to this day. Once this sort of monasteries, set up by Christian Albanians emigrating to Italy, flourished in Italy, today San Nilo, counting a dozen monks, is the only one left in Italy but is considered a historical monument and protected, meanwhile attracting many tourists.

Frascati, some 20 km to the south-east of Rome, is in the so-called Castelli Romani regional park of Lazio, and 'castelli' (castles) rather than castles refers to small towns in a hilly setting where the Romans since time immemorial have escaped to for a breath of fresh air and peace away from bustling Rome. We arrive in Frascati, home to about 22,000 souls, just after midday, the bus takes us to the town's main square, there's a colourful street market in course, being a sunny day it's packed with tourists and locals wandering around, rummaging at the stalls, enjoying an ice-cream or having a break sitting on benches and watching the passes-by. To our right I notice a beautiful old villa perched on a mound with huge landscaped gardens. I took in all this within a matter 30 seconds, the bus I hoped would stop, let us get off and stroll around before heading for lunch to a restaurant nearby. Not so, the driver following Luigi's instructions drives around the square and parks about 500 metres from the square, the restaurant is a few minutes' walk away and everybody seems to be a lot more interested in getting down to lunch.

Lunch is at a locally renowned establishment called, Osteria Fraschetta Trinca, that specialises in the regionally renowned dish, porchetta, boneless, fatty pork stuffed with garlic and herbs and roasted on a spit for some eight hours. Having already eaten a meat dish twice on this trip, Nadia and I pass on the porchetta, we have tasty local cheeses, homemade bread and vegetable preserves instead. The Swiss couple sitting next to us suggest we skip dessert and go visit the town for half an hour. Agreed.

We stroll around the street market, gaze up at the Baroque church in the nearby square, take a look at the villa in the distance and learn that it is Villa Belvedere one of 12 such lavish buildings in the area constructed starting 16th century for various popes, cardinals and nobles in Rome. Being lunch time on May 1st, all the town's eateries seem to be packed to the full, if we hadn't booked at our Osteria, equally packed with diners, it would have been hard to find a table. The atmosphere is relaxed, noise is down, views into the countryside placating, I can understand why Romans have been coming to the area for over two millennia.

We catch up with the rest of the group who seem very pleased to have had a hearty, tasty lunch, when we enquired what the dessert consisted of, Michela took out a biscuit of sorts and gave one to us, "I saved it for you," she said, we didn't really miss much. Back on the bus we drove to our next destination, the historical town of Ariccia situated on top of a hill flanked by two deep valleys; around mid-19th century a double-arched bridge 312 metres long, 72 metres high was built to connect the town with Via Appia and end its relative isolation from the main road network in Lazio. From the car park where the bus stopped, we could see the famed bridge towering over our heads, we wondered how we would rise 72 metres to enter the town, no problems, we can take a lift or just walk up the walkway created for the purpose, half the group decided to use the lift, we were among those who chose to walk, not as hard as it first seemed. Our main destination here is the 17th-century Palazzo Chigi framing one side of a handsome square apparently designed by Lorenzo Bernini.

The atmosphere in the town seems quite relaxed, many are sitting at outdoor cafés chatting away, a few cars drive past unhurriedly. We stand before the imposing Palazzo Chigi, essentially a Baroque building but its symmetry and rationalist design are already hinting at Neoclassic architecture that would soon be fashionable in 18th century. Our guide, a twenty something brunette, informs us about the history of the palazzo interjecting entertaining anecdotes here and there. Savelli family, the feudal lords of Ariccia, built the first palazzo which was taken over by Chigi family in 1661 and had it rebuilt and expanded by Carlo Fontana, Bernini's disciple, to its current state and size. The Chigi sold the palazzo to Ariccia municipality in 1988 and extensive restoration followed, completed in 1999. Today it is one of few such historical buildings furnished with original 17th-century furniture and decor and houses a series of museums.

Room after room, downstairs and upstairs, splendid frescoes, paintings and furniture including two elaborate sideboards by Bernini are indeed impressive but what sticks most in most people's minds are probably the billiard's room, portraits of 17th-century noble women in daring hair-does perfectly exemplifying 17th-century hair styles in vogue at the time and the sharply contrasting, plain portraits of a series of nuns. The some 400-year old pharmacy also draws the attention. We eventually come to a large hall with large Baroque paintings hanging on the walls, in a small chapel is a small moving fresco by Bernini depicting St Joseph and baby Jesus; the room with rows and rows of 21-stcentury chairs is used for conferences, concerts and more. From the windows we can see the spacious, landscaped gardens extending into the distance but as usual there's no time to linger any longer, we have to be at the bus in 15 minutes. As we emerge from 17th-century splendour of the palazzo we see the perfectly symmetrical church, Santa Maria Assunta, designed by Bernini, opposite beckoning us, no time to go inside though, we take a side road and walk literally to the edge of the town, there's a lively street market in course, safely behind a parapet, we admire the wide landscape extending into the horizon below us, there's hardly any time left, we should be on the bus in five minutes, we run to the walkway and quickly descend to the park, sulky, even angry faces glare at us, we were 10 minutes late, oh dear!

The following day was our last, we said our good-byes to the hotel staff and boarded the bus. We were supposed to visit Castel Gandolfo, a delightful village home to around 9,000 inhabitants on the shores of Lake Albano high up in the hills famed as the summer residence of popes for over four centuries. Luigi announced we wouldn't be going there, the highly popular location was much too expensive to enter, all tour buses pay a fee to gain access to the village centre, as was visiting the pope's palace, Palazzo Pontificio, actually only the gardens are open to the public. A deathly silence ensued, he said we would pay a visit to a Benedictine monastery, Monastero di San Benedetto, in Subiaco, instead, lesser-known perhaps but just as interesting, and free to visit, he also promised we would drive by Castel Gandolfo on the way back, take a look at Lake Albano but won't actually get off the bus, was that OK? Half the people protested, but there was no way of finding consensus, in the end Luigi pulled out a winning card, we each would have to pay extra if we really wanted to go to Castel Gandolfo, and the admission fee to the pope's palazzo (pricey) was not included in the tour package, grumbling finally subsided and in no time we were on our way to Subiaco.

A pleasant enough drive through Lazio's countryside took us to Subiaco but not the town itself, the bus climbed and climbed stopping at a short distance from the monastery, Subiaco itself was facing us across the valley. A brief uphill walk took us to the entrance of the monastery. A monk gave us a guided tour of the solemn edifice, carved out of a steep rock surface, a terraced rose garden softens and embellishes the austere building soaring into the sky, inside is a series of chapels at different levels decorated with truly magnificent frescoes dating back to 8th century including a famed one of St Francis painted in 1223, considered the oldest portrait of the saint, when he came for a visit. Isolated, almost invisible among the hills, this is where St Benedict came to live in a cave as a hermit in 6th century, the cave is still there. There is always, it seems, someone sitting or standing inside the small cave in deep contemplation. Benedict founded the earliest monasteries for spiritual retreat and meditation, he later founded many other monasteries which were taken as models for all monasteries in Europe. The monastery here began expanding in 11th century finally taking its current shape and size, a simple austere building style renders it almost invisible to the eye as if it is growing out of the rock. In the refectory is a recently restored Last Supper fresco realised in 13th century making it more than two centuries older than Leonardo da Vinci's masterpiece in Milan.

    How time flies, it's nearly lunchtime, we take a short drive to an offshoot of Subiaco monastery functioning as a guest house, bar, restaurant and souvenir shop to have our packed lunches quickly and head for home, it's a long drive. The guest house bears St Benedict's motto, Ora et Labora (prey and work), we had no intention of doing either, some bought liqueurs made by the monks, religious trinkets etc. and we settled in the courtyard enjoying the view down in the valley and began munching our cheese rolls, but half the party is missing. A quick enquiry revealed, Luigi and his cronies unilaterally decided to prolong the lunch break from half an hour to whatever it takes to go through a three course lunch, and coffee to follow at the bar upstairs. As 30 minutes became two and half hours, the impatience of those waiting gradually turned from impatience to rage. I was asked to enquire what was taking so long, Luigi meekly explained, as they went upstairs to have coffee, a sizeable group of teenagers barged in and began buying sweets, sandwiches, soft drinks etc which took a good 20 minutes, by the time Luigi and friends had their coffee 20 more minutes flew by. This little-convincing excuse made the group waiting even more furious, we urged them to get on the bus, we had a long way, we were supposed to arrive in Como around 9 p.m. and had onward journeys, everyone's plans were obviously going to be disrupted.

Amid much complaining and discontent the bus lurched forward only to stop after five minutes, we must have covered no more than a few km. One of the diners forgot his camera in the restaurant and Luigi was on the phone trying to arrange it with the waiter to bring it to us to the bus. After 15 minutes of waiting, Luigi came towards us to apologise for this further delay, the calm, peace-loving Swiss couple sitting behind us began throwing abuse at him for his incompetence and pathetic organisation wasting everyone's time first with the long lunch break only half the people agreed to, and now causing more delay for the sake of a cheap camera, on day one he had told everyone that if any personal belongings were left in the hotel rooms or restaurants, he would arrange them to be delivered to his office in Como and pass them on to the owners. Luigi seemed truly stressed, stuck between two fires, I felt sorry for him. "I presume you won't be joining us on our next trip," he commented, "but I guarantee you, nobody can beat us for the price." This drew even more abuse, not only from the Swiss couple.

The return trip, with a toilet break halfway to Como, proceeded with subdued moods at the back of the bus but quite merrily at the front where most of the those who opted for the long lunch break sat, this upbeat mood was probably catalysed by conspicuous wine consumption back at the monastery. Luigi made no more announcements about upcoming trips he had planned. Needless to say we arrived in Como nearly three hours after the scheduled time. As we got off the bus, Luigi came up to me and shook my hand, apologised for all the delays and 'unforeseen' deviations from the tour itinerary, I probably surprised him by kindly thanking him for all his effort to keep everyone happy, he hugged me and said a heartfelt good-bye knowing we would probably never meet again.

As we approach the end of this book, how can I put a full stop and retire so to speak? The 22nd, and last chapter, will indeed be on the theme of retirement; how and when do Italians retire from work, how much of a pension do they get, what do they do once they've retired?

TWENTY-TWO

RETIREMENT IN ITALY

Ever since Italian government led by Mario Monti introduced sweeping pension reforms late 2011, retirement has become one of Italians' most popular topic of conversation. With the new legislation already approved by both the senate and the chamber of deputies, the retirement age was raised to 66 starting Jan. 2012. Until Dec.31, 2011, all employees and the self-employed could retire with a full pension, regardless of age, if they'd paid contributions for at least 40 years. All Italians were, however, eligible for an old age pension, regardless of any contributions, once they'd reached the age of 60 for women, and 65 for men. Monti government changed the rules here too, the right to receive this minimum pension, currently around €550 a month, is to be maintained but the age is to be gradually increased to 66 for both men and women by 2018. Known as Legge Fornero, after the minister Elsa Fornero, this pension reform for the first time is allowing Italians to continue working up to the age of 75, if they wish, and increase their contributions before they finally retire for good. Come 2017, ISTAT reported that life expectancy of Italians increased by five months, 85 years for women, 80.6 for men, and the retirement age was delayed further, to 67 years, up from 66 years seven months, starting January 2019. Trade unions vehemently protested arguing workers doing arduous jobs should retire earlier. Government finally gave in and exempted 15 categories of such workers including primary school teachers, nurses, construction workers, farmers, fishermen and steelworkers who can retire after 38 years of work and reached the age of at least 63.

Why this dramatic change? Italy, like many other European nations, has been through a biting financial crisis; there's been little growth in recent years and till 2014 the economy actually continued contracting. At the time of Monti's pension reforms Italy had the largest debt in the 28-member European Union (EU) after Greece, standing at around €1.93 trillion in Mar. 2012, corresponding to 123% of GDP (gross domestic product), Bank of Italy informed. That figure continued going up in the following years reaching €2.21 trillion in Jan 2015, and €2.28 trillion in 2017. Along with raising taxes, VAT and fighting widespread tax evasion, the government had to cut pensions too bearing in mind in 2012 the state paid over €270 billion to pensioners; a huge sum representing some 15% of GDP.

Although retiring at the age of 65 or 66 is quite normal in EU and beyond, it came as a bit of a shock to Italians used to generous state pensions. Between 1973 and 1992 women working for the state had the best pension options: after 14 years 6 months and 1 day of work they could retire to family life; men in the same conditions worked 5 more years and all those employed by the municipalities could retire after 25 years of work. This produced a mass of pensioners in their 30s and 40s. Today, the state is still paying pensions to around 428,800 retirees under the age of 50 which is costing the tax payers €7.4 billion a year, as reported by the census bureau ISTAT and INPS, the institute of national social security. The employees working in the private sector and the self-employed had to work for at least 40 years before they could retire which still meant millions of people quitting work and earning a pension long before the age of 65. That's not all, on top of pensions Italian state also helps disabled persons, depending on degree of disability, and family income, everyone gets state aid; those under 18 receive more generous aid which can vary from €500 to €900 in cases of 100% disability. The disabled deemed 100% incapacitated like the blind between the ages of 18 and 65 receive a monthly check of €260. It's worth noting that in Italy nearly all workers and pensioners also get a *tredicesima*, a thirteenth salary, in December, not necessarily to spend on Christmas presents!

How did it all start? As industrialization began in early 19th century, people started moving to the cities; the large, extended families in the countryside who cared for each other gradually gave way to nuclear families, and in the case of the bread earner, almost always a man, falling sick, losing his job or getting old and eventually dying, the wife and children were left without any means to care for themselves. Against this serious social issue, in mid-19th century workers associations for mutual help known as, *Le Società di Mutuo Soccorso*, were formed. In 1862, a year after united Italy was born, some 440 such associations existed in central and northern Italy; workers joined them voluntarily and paid a regular contribution. In 1882, finally the state stepped in and set up an insurance fund against accidents at the work place, again workers could participate on a voluntary basis. In 1898, this insurance was made obligatory and more importantly still, a national security system called *Cassa di Previdenza* was set up to care for the disabled and elderly but workers were allowed to choose whether they wanted to pay a percentage of their salaries in exchange for this service. The state as well as the employer made a small contribution to the pensions matured marking the beginning of the current system. In 1904 it became obligatory for state and railroad workers to join the *Cassa di Previdenza*; in the ensuing years the service was extended to some workers in the private sector too. By 1918 there were 700,000 members and 20,000 pensioners protected by the newfound social security umbrella. The following year insurance against old age became compulsory for all 12 million Italian workers hence everyone was guaranteed an old age pension. The massive re-organization required was handled by a newly created, much larger body, *Cassa Nazionale Delle Assicurazioni*, which evolved into INPS in 1943 everyone is familiar with today.

How does INPS work? It is a state run welfare institute, workers today pay a portion of their monthly salary into a general, national pension plan, the state runs this plan or account and pays the pensions of all the retirees. To qualify for a pension, workers have to make contributions for at least 20 years, for a full pension they have to work for 41 years starting Jan. 2012, as of 2018 men needed to work 42 years 10 months and women a year less to qualify for full pension, and alas, starting Jan. 2019 men will have to work for 43 years and three months and women a year less for the same privilege. For how long this state-run system will carry on working successfully, as it has done till now, is hard to tell. According to ISTAT and UN, Italy will continue to age, it already has the oldest population in EU, and come 2030 about a third of the population will be made up of pensioners over 65. This, however, isn't necessarily going to happen; Italy is accepting migrant workers in increasing numbers for obvious economic necessity. These new Italians who also have more children than Italians themselves are now making a healthy contribution towards paying the pensions of Italy's retired, needy population. Meanwhile, Prime Minister Mario Monti's government of technocrats, not politicians, was looking forward optimistically, "With the reforms already in act and the continuing austerity measures, Italy will make it in a bigger and better way than others in EU," said Monti late Apr. 2012. Corrado Passera, the minister responsible for economic development, supported this prediction, "In the short and medium-term, we'll be spending €100 billion to stimulate the economy, we may well see growth figures turning positive even in 2012." He was partly right there, things didn't turn out that way, to witness economic growth Italians had to wait 2015 but at least serious pension reforms helped improve the state coffers, reforms introduced by Renzi, and his successor, Gentiloni government, in 2017 Italian economy grew by 1.6% as reported by ISTAT in Dec. 2017.

How much does an average Italian pensioner earn these days? ISTAT figures for 2014, the latest available, counted around 16.3 million pensioner, on average they take home earn €17,000 per annum or €1,140 a month after taxes, but a closer look reveals around 8 million pensioner were earning under €1,000 a month and over 13% less than €500 a month. In 2016 these pensions hardly improved, someone earning a salary of say €1,700 before taxes in 2011 was earning €1,742 in 2016. Meanwhile there's a privileged group of 33,000 individuals, mostly politicians, high ranking army and navy officials and state-owned company managers who receive over €90,000 per annum, before taxes, costing INPS €3.3 billion a year. Referred to as 'Pensioni d'oro' (golden pensions) they're often in the news being blamed for this privilege, Renzi's government responded by bringing in legislation to limit pensions to 80% of last salary earned just before retirement.

So many retirees earning a pension bearably enough to get by, if at all, is not a new problem; employees who can afford it, buy private pension plans to supplement their state pension, a number of professional categories like journalists, doctors, lawyers, managers have their own associations who run a pension fund on their behalf and on retirement get an extra pension on top of their state pension. Still, this leaves out a big chunk of workers who only get a state pension and with the recession that hit the economy producing high numbers of unemployed meant these workers are now unable to make 40 years of contribution and wait till they're 66 to get a pension as required by the Fornero reforms. What further frustrates the situation is that if someone loses their job in their mid or late fifties, they're unlikely to find a new one. Giuliano Poletti, the employment minister, aware of the social problem this may cause, proposed a certain degree of flexibility to help these needy citizens. One seriously being considered in Jan 2015 was allowing people who've made 35 years of contribution to get a pension when they turn 62 but accept a reduction of their pension by 8% at the most.

Starting with Expo Milano in 2015 that acted as a powerful stimulus for Italian economy, more growth, more jobs have been created and state accounts improved and curbed at times crippling cuts; With the economic upturn in course, Italy's pensioners old and new look forward to a better future; what lies in the distant future is hard to tell for anyone but prospects for the foreseeable future seems bright; hopefully Italians will seize the opportunities opening up and confidently march ahead, and enjoy life, at least for the time being.